Marilyn Vancil has really done something here. Looking at the personality types of the Enneagram through the lens of scripture and solid Christian theology, she emerges with a very helpful tool. Clearly written and focused, her down-to-earth applications and recognition of human complexities are refreshing and honest. Any pastor, counselor, or person will benefit from reflecting on how we perceive ourselves and others, and what gets in the way of being the people God created.

—Dan Baumgartner, Senior Pastor
Hollywood Presbyterian Church

In *Self to Lose - Self to Find,* Marilyn presents how our personality pattern relates to our path of development and liberation in relationship to God. She provides a thoughtful and ground-breaking analysis of the Enneagram system and its valuable contribution to the work of development in the Christian life.

—David Daniels, M.D.
Developer of the Enneagram in the Narrative Tradition.

I've been waiting for this book! Several years ago, Marilyn Vancil facilitated a workshop at our annual married couples' retreat and we still talk about it. As she unpacked the Enneagram for us, "aha moments" resounded as we considered its application and implications for ourselves and our marriages. *Self to Lose - Self to Find* is such a valuable resource! This wonderful book simplifies the Enneagram, combines it with scripture, and communicates practical ways it can be applied to daily life.

—Jonathan Schultz
Director of Alumni and Friends, Young Life

Incredible wisdom, depth of understanding, and life-changing insights into your very being are some of the amazing gifts you will receive as you turn these pages! This is a treasure-trove of practical guidance that will equip you to live more congruently as the *authentic* person God created you to be.

—Glenna Salsbury, Professional Speaker
Author of *The Art of the Fresh Start* and *Heavenly Treasures*

Neither the Myer-Briggs sorter or Gallup's Strengths Finder can match the spiritual, psychological, and emotional treasure in this book—it's that good!

—Mick Silva, Editor and Blogger
MickSilva.com

SELF TO LOSE
SELF TO FIND

———

SELF TO LOSE
SELF TO FIND

—

A Biblical Approach to the
9 Enneagram Types

MARILYN VANCIL

REDEMPTION
PRESS

ISBN 13: 978-1-68314-038-2 (SC)
978-1-68314-039-9 (HC)
978-1-68314-040-5 (ePub)
978-1-68314-041-2 (Mobi)

Library of Congress Catalog Card Number: 2016938133

To Mom and Dad,

Your generous and faithful love

anchored my life

and gave me the confidence to try anything.

Like daring to write a book!

Thank you!

"The more we let God take us over, the more truly ourselves we become—because He made us. He invented us. He invented all the different people that you and I were intended to be. . . . It is when I turn to Christ, when I give up myself to His personality, that I first begin to have a real personality of my own."

—C. S. Lewis

TABLE OF CONTENTS

Section Four: Practicing a Path to Freedom

GRATITUDES

My heart overflows with gratitude for the many people who have blessed me with their love, support, wisdom, and encouragement throughout my life and during the writing of this book. Thank you to each person who voiced enthusiasm for this project. Without you, this would have remained just a flickering idea.

Thank you Jeff...my dear husband of forty four years. Your constant love for me and your belief in God's message through me gave me the courage to keep pressing forward. Thank you for the countless ways you allowed me time and space to create. Your wisdom, insights, and passion for the scriptures provided me with much-needed guidance. I love and admire you more than anyone on earth and am beyond grateful for our life together.

Thank you Kristen, Emily, JJ, and Kurt...my precious children...for cheering me on. You continue to inspire and teach me by how you live and love. It has been my greatest joy and honor to be your mom. Thank you Ryland, Jason, Katy, and Leslie...my children-in-law...I'm so grateful you joined our family. And, to my delightful grandchildren...may you always know how much you are loved and treasured by your Mimi.

Thank you to my praying girlfriends...those who received and responded to my "morning memos" by offering prayers on my behalf and sending me such loving notes of encouragement. Knowing that you were on my team kept me going when I wanted to quit and bolstered my confidence when I needed it most.

Thank you to those who provided a sacred space for me to write…Martin and Beth Barrett, Mark and Terri Judy, and Tom and Diane Ruebel. My times of retreat into the quietness and beauty of your holy places birthed many of the ideas and images found here.

Thank you Nancy Rowland and Linda Snyder for reading through my drafts and offering your thoughtful feedback and wise counsel.

Thank you to all those who shared their personal reflections and real-life experiences with me. Hearing how your Enneagram pattern influences how you live was a key factor in how I presented each type.

Thank you to my many mentors and teachers, both directly and indirectly, who shaped both my spiritual life and my understanding of the Enneagram and its value for personal growth. Your knowledge and experience are woven throughout this book. I am especially grateful to Dr. David Daniels for permission to include *The Essential Enneagram Test* as a valuable resource for my readers.

Thank you Mick Silva…my editor extraordinaire. You were an answer to my desperate prayers and I am deeply grateful for your immediate excitement about my book idea. Thank you for your expertise and direction as my writing took shape and for constantly reminding me of the value of this work and this message.

Thank you Frank Kremer of square:design online for your talent and support in creating the cover design.

Thank you Athena Dean Holtz and the team at Redemption Press…for your professionalism and masterful skills at taking my manuscript, honoring my voice, and leading me all the way through to publication.

And, I'm filled with deep gratitude to God…for your love and grace poured out to me, for your presence with me always, for trusting me with this calling, and for guiding me every step of the way.

GETTING STARTED

The enney-a-what?
It looks like a New Age symbol.
Is it biblical?
What does this have to do with Jesus?

These were just some of my negative reactions when I was first introduced to the Enneagram thirty years ago through a series of cassette tapes. The cover had a mysterious circular symbol with numbers and criss-crossing arrows. The presenter was someone I had never heard of at the time and it looked like some sort of New Age teaching. I was not at all interested in listening to them and was even cautious. But a trustworthy friend had recommended the tapes, so I gave them a try.

I was immediately hooked! I bought every book I could find on the subject and devoured all of the information. I was astounded at how accurately this personality system described me and other people in my life. I remember reading with tears streaming down my face because I felt known and accepted at such a deep level. I finally made sense and others in my life made sense too. Thus my passion for the Enneagram was fueled and has not let up.

Although this personality system has been an invaluable part of my life's journey for the past thirty years, I've also searched for answers to two crucial questions: 1) How does it support my desire to follow Jesus? and 2) How does its knowledge line up with the teachings of the Bible?

As I studied both the Scriptures and the Enneagram, I discovered correlations that have been liberating and life-changing for me, especially in learning that Jesus invites us to let go of one self in order to live into our true self. My personal quest and my understanding of these correlations form the inspiration and foundation for this book. My hope is that others, particularly those who embrace the teachings of Jesus and desire to follow Him, will find a similar value for their spiritual journey by exploring the Enneagram through a biblical lens.

This model is unlike any other personality typology. It taps into our deeper story, going below the surface of outward behaviors, social styles, strengths and weaknesses, traits and talents. It sheds light on our inner motivations, ardent longings, and deep sufferings. It reveals the filters through which we view life and how these influence the choices we make. It clarifies ways we are held captive by habitual patterns of thoughts, feelings, and actions that we aren't even aware of or can't seem to change. Most importantly, it illuminates our true essence as one who has been created in God's image and how our distorted beliefs and ingrained strategies hinder the full expression of who God designed us to become. If we allow the knowledge offered by the Enneagram to help us know ourselves more clearly, it becomes like a microscope on our inner life, revealing parts we might not recognize or comprehend without a tool to help us take a closer look. And, our inner life matters because this is where true transformation takes place.

It's a strange name for a personality system. *Ennea* is Greek for nine and *gram* means a drawing, so the name simply means "nine drawing." It's a circle with nine numbered points and each number represents a distinct personality pattern or type. The actual circle and the arrows between the points illustrate the interconnections between the different styles. Even the space in the middle has significance. All of this will be explored in more detail throughout the book.

The Enneagram, as it is known today, is an accumulation of ancient spiritual teachings and current psychological research. Early forms come from the teachings of the Christian desert fathers and mothers of the fourth century who recognized various *personality obstacles* that kept spiritual seekers from experiencing wholeness and freedom of life with God. One of these desert elders, Evagrius Ponticus, named eight so-called passions of human nature that later became the familiar "seven deadly sins" in the Catholic tradition. These original eight passions are represented on the circle, with the passion of fear being added later. Over time, other spiritual teachers and human behavior experts contributed to the personality typology we have today.[1] As a result, it is not a proprietary system and is open for varied uses and interpretations. My desire through this book and in my work is to return to its original spiritual roots as a way of understanding and releasing the obstacles that prevent us from living the abundant life Jesus offers.

Frankly, I'm less interested in the origins and history than I am in its validation by countless real-life experiences, both my own and those of others. When something rings true and is confirmed by personal applications in my everyday life, then I take notice. Does it make sense? Does it work? Does it inform me about who I am and how I live? Does it help me become more loving and free? For me, this system has and does. It also does for a vast international community of Enneagram enthusiasts. As the saying goes, the proof is in the pudding.

So how has the "nine drawing" helped me? Four words sum up my personal experience: comfort, compassion, confession, and consent.

First of all, this knowledge has been a source of comfort for me. When I first listened to those tapes and continued to learn, something opened up in me and I felt known in a new way. I was shocked at how my own life experience was described with such accuracy and I was relieved to learn that I actually had a personality! It was comforting to have words and reasons for the angst I was feeling at the time. It was also reassuring to realize that there are others who share the same struggles, quirks, and vulnerabilities.

I've been comforted by recognizing that I'm not as confusing or as "messed up" as I sometimes seem to be; I just have a certain personality type with particular challenges and shortcomings. This is far easier to address than an overarching air of perplexity about myself.

As I continue to make discoveries about my type for personal growth, I often experience what I call "holy aha moments." When I'm in the middle of emotional pain or mental anguish or difficult relational dynamics, I prayerfully consider how my personality pattern might be playing out in my struggle. Often an insight will emerge that settles and comforts me. Clarity about how my type is influencing my negative and restrictive reactions allows me the freedom to let them go. I can then face my current circumstances with a more open heart and mind.

Along with finding comfort, I have grown in compassion for myself. I'm able to look through a lens of kindness and patience rather than a lens of judgment and self-defeat. Knowledge of my type helps me sort out the subconscious messages that drive my fears and insecurities and overreactions, all of which create ways of suffering for me. I can hold this suffering with more tenderness and allow my deeper story to come forth and have a voice. I can also laugh at my idiosyncrasies and not take myself so seriously, accepting that "Ah, yes, there I go again." In this space of compassion for and understanding of myself, there is more room for the love and grace of God to penetrate my life.

I've also grown in compassion for other people. They have a deeper story too. What I see on the surface is not the whole picture. This system has helped me realize that each person interprets life through a filter of underlying fears, distorted beliefs, losses, and desires that may be very different from my own. I believe everyone has a deep yearning to express and experience the image of God imprinted on their souls and is sabotaged by the particular temptations and trials of their type. We all long to live freely, but our habitual personality patterns keep us bound. I see this all the time in my work as a spiritual director and coach. Knowing that we share this human dilemma fosters greater compassion and acceptance in me for all people.

Working with this system has improved my marriage by expanding compassion and grace in our relationship. When my husband, Jeff, and I listened to the original tapes, we were amazed by all the "holy aha moments" about each other. Our struggles to communicate and connect finally made sense. We loved each other and worked at our marriage, but we were in a vicious cycle of hurting each other and feeling misunderstood. We would hash out an argument, defend ourselves, choose to forgive, and resolve to make some changes. But the same cycle would repeat itself. When we discovered and accepted that we both had very different inner stories and motivations, the lights went on. No wonder we misunderstood each other; we were misinterpreting each other all the time.

The Enneagram continues to be a reference point we turn to when we're at a standstill in our marriage and need to be reminded of our different personality patterns and how they impact our situation. For instance, I'm sensitive to ways I feel insignificant and he is prone to perceiving he has failed. I want symbiosis and he needs autonomy. I focus my energy on staying comfortable and he focuses his attention on pressing forward with new ideas. We have internal operating systems that don't always sync. Before learning about our types, these differences felt personal and we thought all would improve if the other would only adopt our own point of view. That never worked. Now we realize we are looking at life through very different lenses, so we're able to accept and trust each other rather than resist and criticize each other. Grace and forgiveness are more possible and more quickly given. Intimacy, or "into-me-see," has increased because we understand and appreciate each other more.

The Enneagram also serves as a tool of confession for me. It shines a light on the inner workings of my personality and the ways I attempt to be my own god. It exposes the secret fears and defenses that permeate just about everything in my life. It's like a mirror on my motivations and strivings, my reactions and avoidances. Through studying this system, I've gained a clearer understanding of what the Scriptures call my "old self," the one I tenaciously cling to for my identity and assumed survival. With this awareness, I'm more open to confessing and owning up to the specific ways I fall short of God's intended purpose through my self-absorbtion and self-reliance.

Finally, knowing the traps common to my type convinces me that my only hope for change is to consent to God's work in my life. I can't change myself. I've tried. The ingrained habits of my old self run so deep that only God can set me free. But I have to let go. Only when I surrender to God's love and good purposes for me can I more fully live into the person I was created to become. Only by consenting to God's transforming presence to change me from the inside out can I then be drawn more freely into the center of my union with Him.

Comfort, compassion, confession, and consent. As you explore this material, I hope similar responses arise for you. Listen for what bubbles up as you learn. What resonates with your inner experience? Do you find comfort in knowing you make sense? Can you hold yourself and others with more compassion and grace? What brings up a need for confession and surrender? And can you consent to God's transforming work to convert your limited inner story to one of freedom in following Him? I trust you will.

Since this personality typology can seem like a puzzle with many pieces, I've formed the framework with four sections: Understanding Our Human Dilemma, Setting the Scriptural Foundation, Exploring the Nine Personalities, and Practicing a Path to Freedom. Although the first two sections are shorter, they are power-packed and crucial for a full comprehension of the last two sections and the purpose of this book. I urge you not to pass over them in your eagerness to discover or read about your type. The overall theme is *experiencing freedom:* freedom from the old self and into the true self, freedom to live fully, and freedom to love deeply. Ultimately, we are able to be free because "if the Son sets you free, you will be free indeed" (John 8:36).

This book represents an accumulation of the many pieces I've gathered from experts in the field, training workshops, books, individual stories, and from my own quest to understand and apply this teaching in my life with Jesus. This is not a comprehensive look at the Enneagram; many excellent resources cover the subject in more detail than you will find here. This is not a theological book attempting to explain God or Jesus and His many teachings. And it's not about understanding the human psyche or offering self-improvement strategies. What I offer here is my understanding and experience of the Enneagram within a biblical context and how I believe it can be of tremendous value for anyone seeking to follow Jesus and His teachings.

My ongoing mission is to present the basics of this personality system in a scriptural, simple, and serviceable way so it can be understood and applied in everyday life. My heartfelt desire is for everyone to know they were created to experience and express the image of God in a unique and holy way. My hope is that as people access the wisdom of this typology within the framework of a scriptural perspective, they will experience more freedom and greater peace. My continuous prayer is that "out of his glorious riches, he may strengthen you with power through his Spirit in your inner being, so that Christ may dwell in your hearts through faith. And I pray that you, being rooted and established in love, may have power, together with all the Lord's holy people, to grasp how wide and long and high and deep is the love of Christ, and to know this love that surpasses knowledge—that you may be filled to the measure of all the fullness of God" (Eph. 3:16-19).

—*Marilyn Vancil*

Section One

UNDERSTANDING OUR HUMAN DILEMMA

1 | A TALE OF TWO SELVES

*"The essence of Christian spirituality is following
Christ on a journey of personal transformation . . .
The distant land to which we are called is the
new creature into which Christ wishes to fashion
us – the whole and holy person that finds his or her
uniqueness, identity, and calling in Christ."*
— David Benner, Sacred Companions

*"I do not understand what I do. For what I want to
do I do not do, but what I hate I do . . . For I have
the desire to do what is good, but I cannot carry it
out. For what I do is not the good I want to do; no,
the evil that I do not want to do—this I keep doing."*
—Romans 7:15, 18-19

We live in a quandary. On one hand, we embrace God's indwelling
love and presence that will transform us from the inside out. We
taste the freedom of trusting Him to meet our deepest longings.
We experience the true abundance, resonant peace, and grounded
wholeness that come from abiding in Jesus, and we desire to follow
Him wherever He takes us.

Yet like the apostle Paul in the Scripture above, we are perplexed.
We want to do right but don't do it. And we do things we resolve
not to do. Do you relate to this? I sure do. One instant I'm focused
and the next I'm wandering. One minute I'm patient and the next

I'm seething. I embark on self-improvement plans and they never last very long. This is baffling. It's as if two people are living in my one body. I assume this sounds familiar.

An adaptation from Charles Dickens' famous classic *A Tale of Two Cities* aptly describes this human dilemma: "There is the best of me, there is the worst of me, there is the wise me, there is the foolish me, there is the me who believes, there is the me who doubts, there is the me who is in Light, there is the me who is in Darkness, there is the me who hopes, there is the me who despairs, there is the me with everything ahead, there is the me with nothing ahead, there is the me who looks to Heaven, there is the me who looks the other way. . . ."

This is our tale of two selves. John Ortberg puts it this way: "You are your own nemesis, your own biggest problem, because there is a relationship between the best version of you and the worst version of you. What they have in common is that both of them are *you*."[2]

These two selves are referenced in several scriptures. The apostle Paul termed them the old self and the new self, one to put off and one to put on. "You were taught, with regard to your former way of life, to put off your old self, which is being corrupted by its deceitful desires; to be made new in the attitude of your minds; and to put on the new self, created to be like God in true righteousness and holiness" (Eph. 4:22-24).

"You have taken off your old self with its practices, and have put on the new self, which is being renewed in knowledge in the image of its Creator" (Col. 3:9-10).

Jesus spoke of two selves in the primary passages we will consider throughout this book: "Whoever wants to be my disciple must deny themselves and take up their cross daily and follow me. For whoever wants to save their life will lose it, but whoever loses their life for me will save it. What good is it for someone to gain the whole world, and yet lose or forfeit their very self?" (Luke 9:23-25). Jesus seems to be saying that we have a "very self" which differs from the self we are to disown. In other words, there is a self to lose and a self to save. This requires some contemplation.

Many spiritual teachers, from ancient times to modern day, name these the "false self" and the "true self." In his insightful book *The Deeper Journey*, theology professor M. Robert Mulholland explains the importance of understanding these two selves in the Christian spiritual life: "There are two fundamental ways of being human in the world: trusting in our human resources and abilities or a radical trust in God. You cannot be grasped or sustained in the deeper life in God—being like Jesus—until you are awakened at the deep levels of your being to this essential reality . . . Unless you are aware of these two selves, these two ways of being in the world, you will have difficulty allowing God to lead you into a deeper life of wholeness in Christ."[3]

As I've contemplated the reality of these two selves and sought to distinguish between them in my own life, I've adopted two titles that are easier for me to get my head around: The Adapted Self and the Authentic Self.

I understand the notion of adapting, adjusting, accommodating. The worst self, false self, or old self develops out of our need to adapt to the world in which we live. It's the self we come to believe we have to be in order to survive and have our basic needs met. It's the *self to lose*.

I also get the idea of being authentic, real, and genuine. Our best, true, new self is the one created to reflect God's image in a unique way. It's the deeper self made to be in union with Him. It's the self that longs to emerge through the layers of our Adapted Self in order to experience and express our original design. It's the *self to find*.

Whatever terms we use, it's crucial for our spiritual growth to acknowledge the reality of our two selves and the dilemma we face as we ask the universal question, "Who am I really?"

One Halloween our grandson expressed this human dilemma quite adamantly. He was dressing in his very thin Transformer robot costume and his mom insisted he wear it over his own clothes before heading out into the cold. He protested. The argument persisted until he finally shouted, "If people see my regular clothes sticking out they will know that I'm just a little kid in a costume!" As we held back our laughter, we also realized he had proclaimed something profound. For him, he was both an imaginary Optimus Prime and a real boy. For us, we seem to embody two identities at the same time, one that is pretend and one that is true.

If these two selves coexist together, how do we discern the difference between our Authentic Self and our Adapted Self?

Perhaps a better understanding of these two selves will help.

2 | THE AUTHENTIC SELF

"We need to find a way to shed our cover, to let go of our ego, to retrieve our original God-gifted selves, to discover the lost treasure of our true persons."

—*Loretta Brady,*
Beginning Your Enneagram Journey

"Therefore there is only one problem on which all my existence, my peace and my happiness depend: to discover myself in discovering God. If I find Him I will find myself and if I find my true self I will find Him."

—*Thomas Merton,*
New Seeds of Contemplation

It's exhilarating and a relief to find something that has been missing.

One time I lost my mother's heirloom ring, one of my most treasured possessions. I searched everywhere in the house. My heart was sick and I was panic-stricken. I vaguely remembered taking it off in the kitchen. I also recalled scooping up food scraps and taking them to the dumpster. I feared the worst . . . my precious ring was lost in the garbage!

With flashlight in hand at 11:00 p.m., I opened the lid and peered inside. The dumpster looked empty. I moved the light to the bottom and there among the food scraps was my ring! I was overwhelmed with relief and joy; I could hardly breathe. I went dumpster diving! My ring had been there the whole time, but I didn't know where it was until I found it.

Jesus often taught about finding things that were lost or hidden. He talked about a wandering sheep, a misplaced coin, and a wayward son that were recovered and the celebrations that followed: "Rejoice with me, I have found my lost sheep. . . . Rejoice with me, I have found my lost coin. . . . Let's have a feast and celebrate. For this son of mine . . . was lost and is found" (Luke 15:6, 9, 23-24).

In another passage, Jesus likened the kingdom of heaven to finding something of great value: "The kingdom of heaven is like a treasure hidden in a field. When a man found it, he hid it again, and then in his joy went and sold all he had and bought that field. Again, the kingdom of heaven is like a merchant looking for fine pearls. When he found one of great value, he went away and sold everything he had and bought it" (Matt. 13:44-46).

And Jesus taught that we would find our true life in Him. "For whoever wants to save their life will lose it, but whoever loses their life for me will find it" (Matt. 16:25).

The Greek word for *find* in all of these Scriptures is *heurisko*, denoting a discovery of some kind, whether by intentional searching or by chance. The word "eureka" comes from this. Archimedes, the renowned Greek mathematician, was supposedly the first to utter it when he realized that his body submerged in a bath would displace the same volume of water. Rumor has it he was so excited about this revelation that he jumped out and ran naked down the street shouting, "Eureka, I found it!"

Archimedes found a truth that was not known to him before. In Jesus' parables, the treasure and the pearl were already there before they were discovered; the sheep, the coin, and the son were somewhere even though they seemed to be lost. My mother's ring was always in the dumpster; I just had to find it.

In the same way, we have a self to uncover that's already there. It's our Authentic Self—the one "created to be like God in true righteousness and holiness" (Eph. 4:24). The one "being renewed in knowledge in the image of its Creator" (Col. 3:10). The one "hidden with Christ in God" (Col. 3:3).

David Benner, in his book *The Gift of Being Yourself,* describes the reality of our Authentic Self this way: "Beneath the roles and masks lies a possibility of a self that is as unique as a snowflake. It is an originality that has existed since God first loved us into existence. Our true self-in-Christ is the only self that will support authenticity. It and it alone provides an identity that is eternal."[4]

Not only is our Authentic Self unique and eternal, it's also the image of God imprinted on each of us. Dick Staub, the author of *About You*, explains this truth:

> What does it mean to be created in God's image? The Hebrew root of the Latin phrase for image of God - *imago Dei* - means image, shadow, or likeness of God. You are a snapshot or facsimile of God. At the very least this means humans occupy a higher place in the created order because we alone are imprinted with godlike characteristics. Your godlikeness is the path to your greatest fulfillment. You will feel the greatest pleasure and wholeness when who God made you to be is fully developed and expressed . . . Furthermore, though all humans possess these godlike capacities, each of us has the potential to express them distinctively, because God's image has been imprinted uniquely on each of us. In God's infinite creativity there are no duplicates; you are the *only* you there has ever been or ever will be.[5]

Isn't that amazing? That our Authentic Self was designed to express God's image in a way only we can do? That we will find our greatest fulfillment in becoming who God created us to become?

Realizing the profound truth that I actually had a *self to find* was a life-changing moment for me a few years ago. I'd been confused about this for a long time. Somehow I thought I was supposed to get rid of everything about myself in order to follow Jesus. You know . . . all of Him and none of me. I knew the teachings about "dying to myself" and I would try to surrender all the parts of me . . . over and over and over. I even had the idea that my ultimate destiny was to become someone different. Yet there was always something pushing through the ground of my very being, trying to make itself known. I tried to dismiss it because, after all, this seemed like the Christian way to live, but I continued to experience discouragement and guilt and a subtle resistance to a God who seemed to discount me.

Part of my confusion had been with the ambiguous phrase "a relationship with God." I wondered what my relationship with God was really supposed to be like. Distant or intimate? Casual or reverent? Warm and fuzzy or fearful and respectful? Was He my friend or my master? I also wondered how and where I relate with Him. Is He out there in the cosmos or within me? Is He always near me or do I need to ask Him to be? And if I have given up claim to myself and have no self left, what part of me is in relationship with Him anyway?

Good questions, don't you think?

While reading *The Deeper Journey* a few years ago, I experienced a holy aha moment that transformed my life and settled this confusion. In his book, M. Robert Mulholland expresses the journey to our true self so beautifully. The following statement, referring to the prayer of Jesus in John 17, penetrated my soul: "Jesus is indicating that the purpose of the Christian life is a loving union with God at the depths of our being."[6] Wow! *A loving union. With God. At the depths of my being.* This means I have a deep being . . . an *Authentic Self* where I am united with Him in love. Eureka!

This revelation was like finding a hidden treasure of truth I'd been missing and it opened up a new spaciousness in me. My mind cleared, my heart lifted, and I felt a deep peace down to my very core. It was exhilarating! I'm not exaggerating. My life with God began a new trajectory that day, one of resting in the reality of my inseparable relationship with Him, rather than thinking I had to dismiss everything about myself in order to know and follow Him.

I finally allowed room for the "something" that had been trying to make itself known in me . . . my true and very real self.

This doesn't mean that everything about me is worth hanging on to, as we shall see in the next chapter on the Adapted Self. I don't always live out of my God-designed self or display the godlike characteristics imprinted on me. Far from it. Yet I know where to return in faith . . . to the center of my loving union with God. It's from that place of trust that God can change me into the one He created to reflect His image. And a critical part of this ongoing journey of transformation is to discern when I am operating from my Authentic Self, united with God, or my Adapted Self, created by me. I believe that's the most crucial awareness we need to develop in order to live fully and freely into our *Imago Dei*. This is where the knowledge of the Enneagram can be so insightful and helpful.

3

THE ADAPTED SELF

"Some of us will wear ourselves out trying to change ourselves before we realize it is not about fixing; it is about letting go—letting go of old patterns that no longer serve us . . . All we stand to lose is the false self—the adaptive behaviors that are ultimately in opposition to the life of love and trust and being led by God that our hearts long for."

—Ruth Haley Barton,
Strengthening the Soul of Your Leadership

"All sin starts from the assumption that my false self, the self that exists only in my own egocentric desires, is the fundamental reality of life to which everything else in the universe is ordered."

—Thomas Merton,
New Seeds of Contemplation

If our Authentic Self is the essence of who we were created to become, then what's the problem? Why don't we live more freely as our Authentic Self? Where are the godlike characteristics we are meant to express? Why does the treasure of our true self seem hidden sometimes? Or most of the time? Because it's covered over by the Adapted Self.

Consider a seed and how it grows into a fruitful plant. I love it when our garden supplies fresh salads in the summer. We enjoy the nourishment from one tiny seed that miraculously sprouts and grows into a head of lettuce. But a lot happens before we can eat it. The intricate process that goes on below the surface serves as a good illustration of the Adapted Self.

A brief biology lesson here. As a seed forms from the mother plant, an outer coat grows around the tiny embryo to cover it until it germinates. This covering is called the seed coat and is made of the same biological material but in a different form. In favorable conditions—like fertile soil, enough water, and the right temperature—the outer seed coat will soften, open up, and allow room for a sprout to emerge and grow into a plant. The seed coat serves an important role of protecting the seed so it will survive and have a chance to be fruitful. However, the protective cover is not the real seed. It will fall away when it's no longer needed and will turn into compost that provides some nutrients for the growing plant. Jesus spoke of this when he said, "Truly, truly, I say to you, unless a grain of wheat falls into the earth and dies, it remains alone; but if it dies, it bears much fruit" (John 12:24 NASB).

Applying this illustration to our lives, the seed coat represents the strategies we adopt early in our childhood to protect our tender lives. These play an essential part in our human development to ensure we survive and blossom. They are not wrong or sinful. It's when we depend on this outer cover for our identity and meaning that we have a problem. We desperately cling to it because we don't know who we are without it. This "seed coat" becomes the false self, an illusory and empty shell. It's not the God-created self but a masquerading version of it. It's what we need to shed in order for our Authentic Self to emerge.

So how and why is this Adapted Self formed?

The Scriptures tell us we are made in God's image. We aren't God, but we are created to reflect Him. Each person is born with a propensity, a hardwiring, that is a particular expression of God's divine nature. It's as if the pure light of God shines through a prism and breaks into a myriad of colors, with each person reflecting a facet of God in a special way. The Scriptures tell us that "since the creation of the world God's invisible qualities—his eternal power and divine nature—have been clearly seen, being understood from what has been made" (Rom. 1:20).

In other words, all of creation is a visible expression of the unseen God. Each blade of grass, tree, sunset, mountain, and creature reveals something of the power and divine nature of God. Since humans are the crowning glory of creation, why would it not be the same for us? In a limited way, you and I are a visible expression of the invisible God. It's an amazing thought!

Having four children of my own convinces me that people come into the world with a bent and a specialty. Each of them displayed different propensities from the get-go. One is attuned to harmony and ease, one is drawn to rightness and order, one is aligned with justice and strength, and one is attracted to nurture and healing. Each is exceptional in his or her own way. We don't come into this world as a blank slate, waiting to be written on. Environmental forces like parents, friends, teachers, circumstances, all flavor the way this hardwiring expands and unfolds. Both nature and nurture matter. But we start with a particular inclination, a leaning, a unique expression of God's character.

We also come into this world innocent, unwounded, and full of wonder. Just stare into the eyes of a newborn child. I think that is why we are so taken with them . . . they remind us of our original state. We see in them a unique and precious connection with the Divine One, and they have complete freedom to be themselves in every way. They do not hold back their expressions, their desires, their needs, their delights. Every parent knows this.

But being born into the world is a shock. From nine months of comfort, provision, and connection, humans are thrust into a world in which they must survive on their own. Even in the best of conditions, parents are flawed and inadequate to meet every need. The world is full of brokenness and wounding. We have an enemy who is out to kill, steal, and destroy the image of God in us (see

John 10:10). We are also born with a survival instinct that serves us, yet pushes us to do what we must to get along in the world. We have inherited the vulnerability and corruptibility that began with the original fall of humanity. And life happens. It just does.

I wonder if the primal cry of the human heart is "Why have you forsaken me?" Do these words of Jesus on the cross echo the sense of abandonment and separation of our human experience? From the moment our umbilical cord is cut, we undergo a loss of connection that we feel deeply. Young infants suffer separation anxiety when they realize they are no longer in union with mom. The fields of psychology and spirituality affirm that we all experience a fear of abandonment. We feel forsaken and separated, from both God and our own true nature, and we spend our lives trying to reconnect with the deepest part of who we are in Him. I emphasize that we *feel* forsaken, not that we actually are. All throughout the Scriptures we see that God has always been for us, not against us. And our true nature created in the image of God is always part of us; it just gets covered over.

Faced with the reality that we are on our own, we figure out what works to assure that our basic needs are met. This is not only about food and sleep and dry diapers, but our deeper needs as well. I came across a little book by Thomas Keating that explains our human beginnings this way: "All of us have been through the process of being born and entering this world with three essential biological needs: security and survival, power and control, affection and esteem."[7]

These three categories make sense. When I pause to ponder what is really going on for me when I'm angry or afraid or insecure in any given situation, I can usually identify that one of these basic needs is threatened. Maybe all three. When I'm irritated that the friendly cashier is chatting with the person in front of me . . . *power and control.* When I change my clothes five times before heading out the door . . . *affection and esteem.* When I obsess over unexplained body pains . . . *survival and security.* Labels like People Pleaser, Worry

Wart, and Control Freak are reflections of these primary needs. As we will see, these three fundamental needs are foundational to the structure of the Enneagram.

As children, we experiment to figure out what works to assure these needs are fulfilled. And we are brilliant at it. We adapt and develop our personalities around our "programs for happiness" as Thomas Keating calls them. And our original hardwiring largely determines what works for us.

As Suzanne Zuercher states in her book *Enneagram Spirituality*, "We begin to create ourselves. We look for and test out those characteristics of mind, feeling, and behavior that will work for us in life. Such decisions and determinations are based on what comes easily and instinctively to us, on what we perceive as being rewarded for."[8]

For instance, if a young child is hardwired to express God's power and strength, he or she will naturally stand up for themselves and others. They will lead the charge on the playground and other kids will follow them and want to be in their circle. This feels good and informs them they need to stay ahead of the pack to be respected and in control. If they experience disrespect or betrayal, the defense system says, "Watch out!" The seed coat of their Adapted Self forms to protect them against injustice and to assure they maintain power and control over their lives by being strong and untouchable.

If a young child is hardwired to express God's nurture in the world, he or she will naturally be inclined to share and care for others and will find satisfaction in doing so. This is met with praise for how unselfish and sweet they are, and it feels really good. This cements in their heart they are loved for their acts of kindness. On the other hand, when they refuse to share or they hurt another child on the playground, they are scolded. This stings and shames them. They perceive they are loved and esteemed only when they act without concern for themselves. The seed coat of their Adapted Self forms to protect their tender heart and to make sure their need for affection and esteem is met by trying to always act selflessly.

Another young child is hardwired to express God's faithfulness. He or she is naturally responsible and drawn to following the rules and obeying authorities. They learn that toeing the line keeps life predictable and they can turn to reliable people for guidance and a steady presence. This is comforting. One day their life is upended when someone they counted on is no longer around. It shakes their sense of security and they wonder who and what they can trust. They come to believe they need to be more diligent so this doesn't happen to them again. The seed coat of their Adapted Self forms to protect their defenselessness and to assure their need for safety and security by worrying and preparing for the worst.

Whichever personal defenses we develop, they serve to protect our tender and vulnerable hearts. This first task in life is unavoidable and is a means of survival. In a way, we "photoshop" ourselves, creating a frame we perceive will get us what we need and want. We modify ourselves and crop what might jeopardize our relationships, our worth, our esteem, our security, and our control. We also add layers of protection. We adapt. And it works. For a time.

Eventually it backfires and no longer serves us.

Since we have fashioned this persona to ensure that our life brings what we want and need most, we cling to it long past its value to us. We rely on this image we've created, yet the outcome of letting it rule us is not so desirable. It turns into defensiveness and resistance. It's the source of anger, fear, and shame. It causes us to bristle and brood, worry and fret. We clamor for attention and validation. We are discontent. We exert power and manipulate. We are independent and stubborn. We become attached to our strengths and minimize our shortcomings. We lose track of our real purpose and strive to please. We sometimes act as if, and even believe, the whole world revolves around us.

Basically, the fruit of our made-up persona is self-centeredness, self-reliance, and self-protection. Sound familiar? Yeah, me too.

Recognition of the Adapted Self is so important that it can't be overstated. When we can admit the reality of this false persona, or seed coat, then we are able to let it soften and loosen its grip on us. When we confess the inadequacy of the Adapted Self to meet our needs, then we can make room for the Authentic Self to show up. As long as we believe we must prove ourselves worthy of esteem, we must ensure our security, and we must maintain control, God's transforming work will be limited.

What is really amazing is that God both creates us with these needs and also fulfills them! Look at the story of creation in Genesis. It still holds true for us today. When God formed humans after creating all the wonders of the universe, He called them "very good." He regarded them with *esteem and affection.* When God told man and woman to "be fruitful and increase in number; fill the earth and subdue it. Rule over the fish in the sea and the birds in the sky and over every living creature that moves on the ground" (Gen. 1:28), He gave them *power and control.* When He said, "I give you every seed-bearing plant on the face of the whole earth and every tree that has fruit with seed in it. They will be yours for food" (Gen. 1:29), He provided the means of *security and survival.*

Isn't that astounding? We don't have to strive for 1) esteem and affection, 2) power and control, and 3) safety and survival. God has already supplied these. What freedom we would enjoy if we lived as if we really believe this. We could let go of our personal programs for happiness, knowing they will never fulfill our deepest needs and desires. We could allow our Authentic Self to break through our protective cover and grow into fruit that will last. Most importantly, just as a sprout grows up when the seed coat softens, roots also go down into the soil to establish a firm hold and a source of nutrients. By relaxing our Adapted Self we can more freely send our roots down into the love and presence of God as the foundation of our being. In doing so, we will find our true identity in Him.

This defines our human dilemma. We live with the conundrum of our two selves, our worst and best versions. In order to grow into wholeness and fruitfulness with God, we must release one to allow the other to flourish. Distinguishing between the two takes prayerful attention and careful discernment. As we now turn our attention to setting the biblical foundation for using the Enneagram, we'll learn from Jesus Himself about how to face and overcome the challenges of our dilemma.

Section Two

SETTING THE SCRIPTURAL FOUNDATION

4

THREE INVITATIONS
FROM JESUS

*"I will give you hidden treasures, riches stored in
secret places, so that you may know that I am the
LORD . . . who summons you by name."*

—*Isaiah 45:3*

*"If you call out for insight
and cry aloud for understanding,
and if you look for it as for silver
and search for it as for hidden treasure,
then you will understand the fear of the Lord
and find the knowledge of God."*

—*Proverbs 2:3-5*

I loved treasure hunts when I was young. My father would set them
up all over the house and he would give us clues to find the hidden
prize. One clue would lead to the next and we raced from place
to place, knowing that we would discover something special like
presents or candy. We trusted that there was a treasure in the end
and the anticipation made it fun. We were willing to "give it our
all" because it was worth it.

Jesus invites us on a similar quest to find treasures about God,
ourselves, and life in general. And He gives us directions about how
to discover them: "If you cling to your life, you will lose it; but if
you give up your life for me, you will find it" (Matt. 10:39 NLT).

"Then Jesus said to them all: 'Whoever wants to be my disciple must deny themselves and take up their cross daily and follow me. For whoever wants to save their life will lose it, but whoever loses their life for me will save it. What good is it for someone to gain the whole world, and yet lose or forfeit their very self?'" (Luke 9:23-25).

According to these words of Jesus, the treasure to find is your life, your very self. He also gives directions on how to find it: deny yourself, take up your cross daily, and follow Him.

In all honesty, I'm not sure Jesus would have made it very far as a motivational speaker with words like these. Deny yourself? Who would want to do that? Take up your cross daily? What does that really mean? The first two instructions aren't very appealing even though following Him may be. It's not like eagerly grabbing clues from my dad and racing to find the prize.

And that's the important piece—trusting that Jesus is inviting us to find a treasure that's worth the cost. These directions are more attractive if we know the end result. If we trust in His good purposes, we might be more willing to comply; when we understand the ultimate destination, then the seemingly difficult directions are easier to embrace.

My dad drew detailed pictures so we could figure out where the clues were leading us, and it's important to look more closely at these key words of Jesus so we can follow them. We'll explore them in more detail, including a look at some original Greek terms used in these passages. As we do, think of them more as invitations from Jesus rather than commands. He invites us to pursue the great treasure hunt of finding our very self in Him. This section will also establish a scriptural foundation for how the Enneagram can be a useful tool in this pursuit.

Invitation #1: Disown Yourself

"And he was saying to them all, 'If anyone wishes to come after me, he must *deny* himself...'" (Luke 9:23, NASB, emphasis added).

Jesus said we must first do something about our self in order to follow Him: deny or disown it.

Let's take a closer look at the meaning of the word most Bible translations use in this Scripture: *deny*. I don't know about you, but self-denial brings up an unwelcome feeling of deprivation, like depriving myself of something delicious or ignoring my heartfelt longings. One dictionary definition for deny is "to restrain oneself from gratification of desires." By applying this understanding of the word to this first invitation, one might conclude that to find the treasure Jesus has for us is a life of saying "no, no, no" to everything we want. In order to follow Jesus, we need to withhold pleasure and suppress our passions. It's either me or Jesus, and there is no in-between. If I want something, it must not be from God.

This is a common and pervasive interpretation of this passage. For instance, one popular Christian writer said it this way: "Your biggest problem is *you*. To follow Christ means you need to learn how to say *no* to *you* . . . deny your wants, desires, and will in exchange for following the wants, desires, and will of the One you are following." Is this what Jesus really meant? Does this sound like the *abundant life* He promised when He came "that they may have life, and have it to the full?" (John 10:10). How can deprivation lead to fullness of life? While there is a place for saying no to one's self, the meaning of this word goes beyond simply dismissing our desires and replacing them with God's, as if these are in complete contrast to each other; as if we are all wrong and must be denied.

A closer look at the Greek word used here gives us more details about this first invitation. The base of the word is *arneomai,* which means "to refuse a person, not to know or recognize him, to reject him, or renounce a relationship." Simply stated, it signifies the denial of a relationship with someone.

This word is also used when Peter denied Jesus prior to His death. In Matthew 26:34, Jesus predicted that Peter would disown Him three times that night. As Peter was recognized as someone who had been with Jesus, he renounced or denied his association with Him, saying, "I don't know him." Peter acted as if he had no relationship with Jesus.

Karl Barth, the highly regarded Protestant theologian, wrote about this in his fourth volume of *Church Dogmatics*:

> Inevitably the man who is called by Jesus renounces and turns away from himself as he was yesterday. To use the important New Testament expression, he denies himself. Where it is used in a pregnant sense, and not merely of a simple denial, *arneomai* always denotes in the New Testament the renunciation, withdrawal, and annulment of an existing relationship of obedience and loyalty. Peter denies that he was ever with Jesus of Nazareth: "I know not, neither understand I what thou sayest."[9] (Mark 14:68)

Here's the crucial distinction: This invitation is less about *depriving* the self and more about *disowning,* or renouncing a relationship with the part of our self that is not what God created us to be.

A similar dismissal of relationship is found in a more disturbing passage in Matthew 7:21-23:

> Jesus said: "Not everyone who says to me, 'Lord, Lord,' will enter the kingdom of heaven, but only he who does the will of my Father who is in heaven. Many will say to me on that day, 'Lord, Lord, did we not prophesy in your name, and in your name drive out demons and perform many miracles?' Then I will tell them plainly, '*I never knew you*. Away from me, you evildoers.'"
>
> (emphasis added)

The Greek word here for *knew* is *ginosko*. According to Vine's Dictionary of New Testament Words, *ginosko* frequently indicates a relation between the person knowing and the object known. So to say "I never knew you" means I do not recognize a relationship or connection with you, similar to the meaning of "deny." These troubling words beg us to wonder: when I get to heaven, will Jesus say "I never knew you?" Even though I tried to follow Him, is it possible that Jesus will deny me? Disown me? Say that He has no relationship with me?

Yet how could He not know me? He created me! He knit me together in my mother's womb. In one psalm we read, "You have searched me, Lord, and you know me. You know when I sit and when I rise; you perceive my thoughts from afar. You discern my going out and my lying down; you are familiar with all my ways" (Ps. 139:1-3).

In considering the whole of God's Word, it seems like He knows us and knows us well. He knows everything about you and me and what we need. We are more valuable to Him than the birds of the air and the lilies in the field. Even our hairs are counted. How could He then say to any of us, especially if we've wanted to follow Him, "I never knew you?"

Maybe it's because *God doesn't know what He didn't create!* What is it that He didn't create? The self or persona that we have fabricated in our own image. It's the seed coat we cling to and rely on for our identity. It's our way of being our own god, which was Adam and Eve's first temptation. It's the self that tries to meet our own needs by our own striving. It's the persona we want others to see to ensure we receive love, find worth, stay safe, and maintain control. It's the Adapted Self.

Judith Hougen in her book, *Transformed into Fire*, says it this way:

> When you believe that the false self is who you really are, then God can know nothing about you, because He recognizes only that which He created. The self that is perpetuated out of woundedness and wrong motives has no meaning, no substance, in the kingdom of God. Its existence is beyond fragile—held together by carefully choreographed thought patterns. It's a dance that adds up to illusion.[10]

This is the self we are to disown and claim no relationship with . . . the one God didn't create.

Karl Barth elaborates further:

> The man who is called to follow Jesus has simply to renounce and withdraw and annul an existing relationship of obedience and loyalty. This relationship is to himself. When he is called to discipleship, he abandons himself resolutely and totally. He can and must say of himself instead of Jesus: "I know not the man" (Matt. 26:72). He cannot accept this man even as his most distant acquaintance.

Therefore, an expanded version of this first invitation might be, "If anyone wishes to come after me, he or she must say *no* to the pretend self, saying, 'I don't know you. You are not the real me.'" We are to disown the self God didn't create, not the one He created and knows intimately.

Our tendency is to lump them together and either hang on to them or dismiss them both, rather than understand their differences and learn to distinguish between them. This involves paying careful attention to how we operate in our everyday lives, so that we can make a distinction between what to disown and what to embrace about ourselves. As we shall see, awareness of one's personality pattern aids this crucial discernment process.

Invitation #2: Take Up Your Cross Daily

"If anyone wishes to come after me, he must deny himself *and take up his cross daily* . . . " (Luke 9:23 NASB, emphasis added).

When people heard Jesus tell them to "take up their cross," they must have been confused and frightened. They knew the implications of this command and it was even more severe than self-denial. When someone took up a cross, they were usually on their way to a common and cruel form of execution. Criminals would trudge through town with a cross over their backs, displaying their shame and guilt before the jeering and angry crowds. These criminals then suffered with their hands and feet fixed to the cross. To take up one's cross meant death.

Two such criminals are mentioned by the gospel writer, Luke. As they took up their crosses, they weren't likely thinking about their plans for the future. They probably pondered the pain ahead of them and their imminent death, perhaps considering the choices they'd made that had led to this day. Two different inner conversations might have sounded like: "I am going to be tortured for my sins. I have hurt others and I'm sorry," or "I don't deserve this. I'm sorry for nothing. And I will never forgive those who got me into this mess."

The two criminals' comments to Jesus indicated two very different attitudes. One admitted he was getting what his deeds deserved. The other mocked Jesus and demanded that He save him. This is a good contrast of the true self and the false self, one letting go of his life and the other clinging to it. One releasing, one demanding. Jesus recognized the heart of the former and promised to be with him in the paradise to come.

As the followers of Jesus heard that they needed to take up their crosses, they only knew it meant death and they had to be willing to die for His sake, which was true. They didn't know the end of the story as we do. They didn't know that Jesus would be crucified and come back to life in a few days. As they later penned the gospel accounts, His command to "take up your cross" would have had more significance and meaning. They understood that though the cross meant death, the final result was restoration and eternal life.

As we consider this second invitation for those who want to follow Jesus, what does it mean for us to take up our cross? How does this apply to us today? How does this invitation lead us to find the treasure of our Authentic Selves in Him?

The apostle Paul often wrote about this: "I have been crucified with Christ and I no longer live, but Christ lives in me. The life I live in the body, I live by faith in the Son of God, who loved me and gave himself for me" (Gal. 2:20).

"For we know that our old self was crucified with Him so that the body ruled by sin might be done away with, that we should no longer be slaves to sin—because anyone who has died has been set free from sin. Now if we died with Christ, we believe that we will also live with him. Count yourselves dead to sin but alive to God in Christ Jesus" (Rom. 6:6-8, 11).

Sin is a confusing, uncomfortable, and misunderstood word. The Greek word for *sin* in the New Testament is *hamartia*, "missing the true goal and scope of life." We have certainly layered more onto this word than this simple yet profound meaning. Sin is not the bad things we do or ways we fail to live up to certain religious standards. Though sin may lead to this, it means first that we miss the mark—the true goal and scope of life that God designed for us. We limit our lives to our own narrow perspective. We cling to the patterns of our Adapted Self rather than the freedom of our Authentic Self.

A familiar Scripture about sin is found in Romans 3:23: "All have sinned and fall short of the glory of God." But what does it mean to fall short of the glory of God by sinning?

I had the honor of making wedding dresses for my daughters and daughters-in-law. In constructing them, only *I* knew how the pieces would fit together. As each of them walked down the aisle, I felt "glory" seeing them in the dresses I had created for this holy moment. It would have been disappointing if they had decided to wear the dresses for another occasion, like washing the car or attending a concert. It would have been heartbreaking if they had refused to wear them for their weddings and had worn jeans and T-shirts instead. They would have "missed the goal and scope" of my intentions.

God has beautiful and unique designs for each of us. He alone knows how the various pieces of our lives will fit together to create a stunning masterpiece. His intention is for us to live as our true self, the unique expression of His image in union with Him, and *this* is what brings Him glory. We "miss the mark" when we live lesser lives, and instead of believing His deep love and holy purposes for us, we cling to our own ways of satisfying our needs. We "aim at other marks" that we think will ensure our safety and security, give us power and control, and earn affection and esteem. In this sense, sin is refusing to put on the true self and living for the old self as if it is all we have. It's using our lives for a lesser destiny than a covenant of love with Him.

The two verses above now take on a deeper meaning. Consider them again here and take note of two selves—one dead, one alive.

"I have been crucified with Christ and I no longer live, but Christ lives in me. The life I live in the body, I live by faith in the Son of God, who loved me and gave himself for me."

"Count yourselves dead to sin but alive to God in Christ Jesus."

The "I" that no longer lives is the self-centered, self-reliant, self-protective one. In Christ, this self is dead and therefore has no power to direct our lives. The seed coat is no longer needed. We are to count on this truth—that our Adapted Self has no life. Thus, to *take up one's cross* is to proclaim, "My made-up self is dead to missing the mark of my original design. It has been crucified with Christ. I will not find real life apart from faith in the One who lives in me. The prideful, independent self is of no use to God or to me, and I claim that it is no more."

The other "I" is the true self, the one in union with God through Christ, the one created to reflect God's image in a unique way. It's the true seed that is meant to flourish and bear much fruit. We are to count on this truth too—that our Authentic Self is alive to God. Therefore, to *take up one's cross* is to also proclaim, "I am made alive in Christ through His resurrection. I am free to become the unique image-bearer that God intended without holding on to the old me that is dead. I am loved unconditionally, I have all I need, and by His power I can experience and express all that Jesus promised."

Is it easy to live out these truths? No way! That is why Jesus said it was daily. Putting to death our habitual and ingrained ways of old-self living won't end as long as we have breath. We will fall short daily and often hourly, clinging to *our* ways of meeting *our* needs and getting what *we* want. We can (and will often) let our false self determine the choices we make. We might even enjoy our self-absorption and the implications of it in our everyday existence. Like one of the criminals who carried his cross next to Jesus, we can hold on to the shell of protection and defensiveness because it seems easier than letting it go.

Or like the forgiven criminal, we can choose a better option. We can count ourselves dead to sin, deserving to die. We can honestly confess our shortcomings, our brokenness, and our guilt from living self-oriented lives. By God's grace, He saves us from the bondage of our self-referential ways and sets us free to more fully experience all that He desires for us. It's an ongoing choice between living in our "ragged clothes" or our uniquely designed "wedding dress."

Invitation #3: Follow Me

"If anyone wishes to come after me, he must deny himself, and take up his cross and *follow Me* . . . " (Luke 9:23 NASB, emphasis added).

The concluding instruction Jesus gave for finding the treasure of our true selves is to *follow Him*. The Greek word here for *follow* is *akolouthe* and is used seventy-seven times in the writings about Jesus' life. It means "to accompany, to express union, to be a likeness, and to go in the same way." If we insert these words into this third instruction, Jesus was saying, "Be with me. Be like me. Go in the same way as I do." This was both literal and metaphorical. Jesus invited specific individuals to physically follow Him wherever He was going and some did. Others did not. He also urged people to follow Him in the greater sense of being like Him. And we are invited to follow Him today by imitating the way He lived.

When you admire someone, you "wannabe" just like them. You watch what they do, how they live. I was once blessed to be under the love and teaching of a woman who exhibited every godly quality I can think of. She was pretty close to being like Jesus. I not only took copious notes during our Bible studies together, I also took meticulous mental notes on how she lived, how she sacrificially served her disabled husband, how she loved and reached out to care for others, how she prayed, how she listened for God's leading in her daily life, and how she lived in freedom to be herself and allow God to minister through her. When we were separated geographically, she wrote me letters and I saved all of them. Her words of wisdom and encouragement and truth always buoyed my spirits and inspired me. They still do even though she's no longer alive. I wanted to be like her by emulating her attitudes, her perspectives, and her trust in God's love and presence in every part of her life. I followed her.

The Bible says in 1 John 2:6: "Whoever claims to live in Him must live as Jesus lived." That's a pretty tall order. How did Jesus live? How can you and I possibly live the same way? Will we walk on water, feed five thousand people with a bit of bread and a few fish, or raise people from the dead? Probably not. But we can study His life and pay careful attention to His words. We can reflect on what characterized His life and teachings and pray for wisdom and courage to apply them to our lives. As I have sought to follow Jesus, two qualities stand out to me: He *let go of His life* and He *freely lived out His destiny.*

The apostle Paul wrote about this to a church at Philippi: "You must have the same attitude that Christ Jesus had. Though he was God, he did not think of equality with God as something to cling to. Instead, he gave up his divine privileges; he took the humble position of a slave and was born as a human being. When he appeared in human form, he humbled himself in obedience to God and died a criminal's death on a cross" (Phil. 2:5-8 NLT).

Cynthia Bourgeault, in her book *The Wisdom Jesus,* elaborates on this Scripture:

> In this beautiful hymn, Paul recognizes that Jesus had only one 'operational mode.' Everything he did, he did by self-emptying. He emptied himself and descended into human form. And he emptied himself still further ('even unto death on the cross') and fell through the bottom to return to the realms of dominion and glory. In whatever life circumstances, Jesus always responded with the same motion of self-emptying—or to put it another way, of the same motion of descent: going lower, taking the lower place, not the higher.[11]

Jesus let go. He did not cling. He relinquished His heavenly privileges by becoming a human and then gave up His earthly life by dying on a cross. During His thirty-three years on earth, there are many examples of Jesus letting go—of possessions, of power, of family, of reputation, of safety, of rights. He humbled Himself in order to serve, love, heal, forgive, and invite people to a life of freedom and abundance. He yielded to His Father in heaven. This cost Him everything. Jesus took the path of descent, of self-emptying. He let go.

And because He did, He was free to live out His destiny. He could fulfill His mission to show humanity what God is like and restore a broken world full of broken people without fear of anyone or anything. He could love openly, live fully, and surrender His life for the redemption of all.

Jesus encouraged people to live the same way. He challenged His disciples to leave their livelihoods, sell their possessions, risk their reputations by associating with Him. He taught the crowds about the blessedness of being poor in spirit, meek, humble, and forgiving. He invited people to love their enemies, turn the other cheek, give away their clothes, and care more for others than for themselves. He told instructive parables about canceling debts, taking the lowest seat, giving without expecting in return, and selling everything to buy one treasure. These commands are also for us today. And there is only one way to fulfill them: let go of the old self we grasp... disown it and count it dead.

This kind of living is counterintuitive. We cling to our identities, positions, rights, and control. Letting go is not very appealing nor is it easy. We naturally resist it. For good reason. We're not sure where it might lead us. Does it mean giving up everything we hold dear or abandoning our dreams? Do we need to give away our possessions and move to a distant land? Do we literally need to die? In the time of Jesus and in many parts of the world today, this truly is the cost of following Jesus. We must not take this reality lightly. For most of us, it's a matter of hanging on to our small selves with all we've got. We resist letting go and we wonder: *what will become of "me" if I fully surrender myself to God?* In our natural minds, it's hard to comprehend that there might be a beneficial result of releasing our protective shell, our seed coat that is familiar and comfortable and seems to serve us so well.

But there is more to letting go than just losing. There is also something wonderful to gain:

> Therefore, God elevated him to the place of highest honor and gave him the name above all other names, that at the name of Jesus every knee should bow, in heaven and on earth and under the earth, and every tongue declare that Jesus Christ is Lord, to the glory of God the Father. (Phil. 2:9-11 NLT)

Letting go leads to experiencing something more. As Richard Rohr puts it, "We overcome evil not by a frontal and heroic attack, but by a humble letting go that always feels like losing. Christianity is probably the only religion in the world that teaches us, from the very cross, how to win by losing."[12] There is a greater gain to letting go.

Jesus was exalted and given a name above all names. He freely lived into His divine destiny. Hebrews 12:3 tells us that because He knew the joy set before Him, he endured the cross. Jesus demonstrated and taught that the path of letting go would lead to something more abundant than the limited life we grasp. He even said that those who humble themselves will also be exalted. That includes you and me if we dare to empty ourselves. He spoke of the freedom, peace, joy, love, and hope found by those who trust and follow Him. He promised a full and free life, not only on this earth but after death. Implicit in His invitation to follow Him is an invitation to trust that He is leading us to a good and spacious place.

To follow Jesus means to adopt the attitude that characterized His life, the attitude of self-emptying, of not grasping, of letting go. It means taking a humble position and relinquishing our self-absorbed ways of living. It requires disowning the Adapted Self to make room for the Authentic Self to emerge. It means taking up one's cross and declaring oneself dead to sin and alive to God. These are not just nice-sounding pious words, but the ongoing challenge of the spiritual journey toward transformation into the unique image-bearer that God created.

How this plays out in our individual and everyday circumstances is the crux of being His follower. Because our Adapted Self and our Authentic Self are not packed in two separate clearly labeled boxes, we have trouble discerning which parts of ourselves we need to disown in order to enjoy the freedom of living out our divine destiny and finding our true self in Him. That's the gift of the Enneagram. As we explore it in the following section, you will discover more specifics on the nature of your personal seed coat and the possible outcomes of letting it go.

A. W. Momerie summarizes the glorious outcome of the invitations Jesus gave as instructions for the treasure hunt toward finding our Authentic Selves:

> The self-denial, then, which Jesus requires of us is not self-de-struction, but self-completion; it is not self-mutilation, but self-development; it is not self-neglect but self-fulfillment. It will bring us gradually to the measure of the stature of the fullness of Christ. It does not ignore any of the various elements of our nature, but it enables them all to work together harmoniously for the perfecting of the whole person. The one who has learned the lesson of self-sacrifice is so changed from what he or she was before this was learned that he or she may emphatically be called a new creature, and yet this one is not less a person than formerly; rather, we should say, it is this one and such as this one alone who really deserves that exalted title.[13]

EXPLORING THE NINE PERSONALITIES

5

THE ENNEAGRAM MICROSCOPE

"To be fully human is to fully reflect God's creative, spiritual, intelligent, communicative, relational, moral, and purposeful capacities. Furthermore, though all humans possess these godlike capacities, each of us has the potential to express them distinctly, because God's image has been imprinted uniquely on each of us."

—Dick Staub,
About You

"Any hope that you can know yourself without accepting the things about you that you wish were not true is an illusion. Reality must be embraced before it can be changed . . . Until we are prepared to accept the self we actually are, we block God's transforming work of making us into our true self that is hidden in God."

—David Benner,
The Gift of Being Yourself

I love the contrast of the two quotes above. We have godlike capacities and we have shortcomings we wish weren't true—that's the tale of our two selves. Like my grandson in his Halloween costume, we possess qualities of both our Authentic Self and our Adapted Self, all in one person.

It reminds me of the first time I looked through a microscope in junior-high science. We gathered items like a hair or a fingernail and mounted them on slides. "*Wow*! *Eew*!" We were fascinated and terrified. It was astounding to discover the intricate structure and cellular activity of these common items. And seeing the mites and dirt on them was disgusting. The microscope revealed and magnified things we could never see with our naked eyes, both hidden wonders and unpleasant realities.

Examining ourselves through the Enneagram lens serves much the same function. If we dare to take a closer look at ourselves in light of our particular personality type, we'll notice both *Wows* and *Eews*. We will see ways we shine and ways we don't; our inherent gifts and our misuse of them; our divinely created genius and how we distort it for our own ends. Each type reflects God's attributes and also exhibits "signature sins" (to borrow a phrase from Michael Mangis' book of the same title[14]). The characteristics of our Authentic Self and our Adapted Self exist together to make up who we are and how we're known.

I recently saw a tattoo on a young woman that read, "When I discover who I am, I will be free." It's so liberating to unlock our inner world and catch a glimpse of our total self—the good, the bad, and the ugly. The Enneagram microscope is invaluable for this quest because it goes beyond outer behaviors to underlying motivations, longings, and barriers. It explains us in ways we may not otherwise know. When I go through the nine types at my workshops, people nod, giggle, and cringe as they hear themselves described so clearly. They also express relief at being known and understood on such a deep level.

It's essential to consider both our *Wows* and *Eews* as part of our transformational journey toward wholeness in Christ. On one hand, when we express our *Wows,* we come alive. In his book *The Me I Want to Be,* Pastor John Ortberg describes the experience of doing something that has a ring of natural talent to it: "You catch a glimpse of the person you were made to be. . . . Only God knows your full potential, and he is guiding you toward the best version of yourself all the time. . . . Flourishing means becoming the person He had in mind in creating you."[15]

On the other hand, a candid recognition of our *Eews* will further our spiritual life as well. Richard Rohr in *The Naked Now,* explains their value:

> Struggling with one's own shadow self, facing interior conflicts and moral failures, undergoing rejections and abandonment, daily humiliations, experiencing your own clear limitations, even accepting that some people hate you: All of these are gateways into deeper awareness and the flowering of the soul.[16]

As we take a closer look at this "microscope," it's important to keep the objective in focus. You may wonder at times where all of this information is leading and of what use it is to you. Think of it as a way to explore your interior landscape. I invite you to view yourself through it with courage and openness. There is no way you can ever plumb the depths of who you are or unravel your complexity, but honest and humble self-awareness will have unmistakable value in your life. As John Calvin wrote in *The Institutes of the Christian Religion,* "There is no deep knowing of God without a deep knowing of self and no deep knowing of self without a deep knowing of God."

The ultimate desired outcome is *freedom*—freedom to love God, love yourself, and love others. *Freedom* for your Authentic Self in God to find new expression. *Freedom* to let go of the obstacles, compulsions, habits, and false identities that hold you captive. *Freedom* to be transformed into the likeness of God you were created to reflect. The purpose is not to alter your personality but to soften it; it's not to make you a different person, but a version of yourself that flows from God's Spirit; it's not to put you in a box, but to identify the box you're already in so you can be free from it.

In preparation for this exploration, first understand that it will create some turbulence—especially inner turbulence—if you take it seriously. It will challenge you beyond your comfort zone. Remember the Enneagram is like a microscope that reveals both *Wows* and *Eews*. An honest look at yourself and the ways you are getting in the way of your personal growth, your relationship with God, and your life with others can lead to some humiliation from what you discover. The type that describes you most accurately is often the one you don't want to see or admit. It can be unsettling to recognize the limitations and lies of the constructed persona you desperately cling to for your identity. But take heart and be patient. It's not all negative. And being able to laugh at yourself is a good antidote. Embrace the reality that this turbulence is necessary for opening a new spaciousness in your inner being. As the seed coat releases, new growth emerges.

Second, be prepared for a lot of information to absorb. I've attempted to keep my explanation of the Enneagram simple and accessible, but it may seem complicated in the beginning. It will begin to make more sense as you keep reading, so just keep going, step by step, and allow the pieces to fall into place. When you're confused and have questions, pause to make a mental note of them and remain curious and open for possible answers as you continue to explore.

Third, keep in mind that my approach to the Enneagram here is to present it as a helpful tool on the journey toward freedom in Christ. Although what I describe is similar to other approaches, it's also unique. The lens through which I look focuses on how this personality profile supports a response to the invitations of Jesus to *disown yourself, take up your cross, and follow Him,* and how it illuminates the "self to lose" and the "self to find" with surprising precision.

Finally, relax and enjoy the journey. May this be a chance to discover and celebrate the real *you* with all of its brilliance and magnificence. May your experience be similar to mine—one of comfort, compassion, confession, and consent as God draws you to the center of His love and the freedom and abundant life of your Authentic Self in union with Him.

The Enneagram Explained

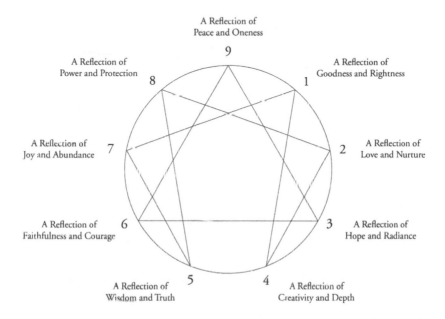

This "nine drawing" has several significant components that work together to comprise the whole system.

First, consider the circle connecting all nine points. Not only is it symbolic of our connection to all the personality types represented by the numbers, it also serves as a picture of the "seed coat" we need to relax and release in order for the true self to grow and flourish. Think of it as the encasement of the Adapted Self that keeps us contained, self-protective, and limited.

Next, draw your attention to the open space in the middle. My friend John Kiemele, the director of a contemplative movement in the Pacific Northwest called Selah,[17] is the only one I've encountered who speaks of the open space in the middle as a representation of our spiritual life with God. As we let go of the traps of the outer circle—our Adapted Self patterns—then we are more freely and deeply drawn toward the spacious center, to the loving union of our spirit with God's Spirit. This is where our true Authentic Self is "transformed into his image with ever-increasing glory, which comes from the Lord, who is the Spirit" (2 Cor. 3:18). As we look at the rest of the Enneagram structure, keep in mind this beautiful, powerful, and expansive open space where God invites us to a life of love centered with Him.

Now look at the numbers around the circle. Each one represents a distinct personality pattern described by common traits and tendencies. In the figure above, notice the divine qualities that identify each type. Various experts have also added representative names for each one (for instance, Riso-Hudson label type Three as "The Achiever," Helen Palmer calls this type "The Performer," and Jerome Wagner uses "The Effective Person."). These labels are helpful to distinguish the particular types. I prefer to use the universal numbers from One to Nine with an emphasis on the divine attributes they embody. Hopefully this is how you can differentiate between them and remember them.

The nine numbers are equal and neutral and have no hierarchical significance. Two is not more valuable than One, nor is Nine higher than the rest. None of the types is better or worse than any other. They each have their contributions and their challenges, their gifts and their limitations. Also, the numbers do not indicate a path of evolution from one to the next.

As you read about the nine personality types in the following chapters, the objective is to determine which one stands out as most descriptive of your life experience and to identify the one pattern most like you. Why? Two reasons: 1) to recognize your "self to lose" and 2) to claim your "self to find" which are both within the same type structure. Remember, the value of this study is to help us more clearly discern the difference between the two and to disown one self so the other has room to emerge. Note this crucial distinction. The Enneagram is not about *defining persons*, but about *describing personality patterns and strategies*. *Defining* restricts ways of explaining yourself and narrows the path of transformation. *Describing* is more open and leaves room for movement and growth.

Determining your particular type requires thoughtful self-observation and reflection. As you read, consider which one resonates most with your inner drives and beliefs. Which one explains the motivations for many of your thoughts, feelings, and behaviors? Which one describes the ingrained habits that block your growth? Which one makes you most uncomfortable, but also has a ring of reality? Which one evokes a sense of suffering? It's natural to focus on the outward manifestations and observable traits, but there is a deeper story within you. Listen for it.

For some people, it will be immediately clear. For others, it will take some time and perhaps much time. You may find that you resemble a few types. This is common as we are a combination of all the types. Sometimes people pick one type and then later realize a different type is more accurate. It's a journey of paying attention to yourself over a period of time, being curious about your reactions to situations, and reflecting on your internal world. It is, most importantly, a matter of prayer and listening to the inner still voice that informs you at a deep level.

One important thing to note is that not everything in the type depictions will apply to you all of the time. And so much more could be said about each type. I hope to simply "prime the pump" for you, so you'll want to delve more deeply into your personality and other resources on the Enneagram. Again, you are looking for the type structure that is *most* descriptive of you.

Here are a few questions I'm often asked:

Are there really only nine kinds of people in the world? Of course not, but we do share some common features with others. Think of the basic colors of red, blue, green, yellow, orange, indigo, and violet, plus black and white. Now think of the last time you wanted to paint something and tried to pick the color you wanted from the options at the paint store. You found unlimited shades to choose from, right? Each tint was a combination of the basic colors—a lot of the main color you wanted and a little bit of this and that to give it a particular hue. In the same way, the nine types are the main "colors," with each type identified by certain beliefs, motivations, strategies, and such. Yet how the type is demonstrated is unique, just like every person is unlike anyone else. You will identify with the characteristics of a particular "color," but the way you express it is exclusive to you.

Are there tests you can take to determine your type? Yes. The one I think is most congruent with the path of self-observation and reflection is from David Daniels' book, *The Essential Enneagram*, which you'll find in the Appendix. The test is designed for use with Daniels' book (which I highly recommend) and particularly in discriminating between the types that seem alike but have underlying differences. For the purpose of my book, this test is offered as a starting point for discovering your type and/or to validate what you notice about yourself as you read through the following descriptions of the nine types. Either way, the demanding work of self-observation is required.

How can you be certain that you have chosen your correct type? Riso-Hudson provide this vivid picture of what it's like when you pinpoint your type:

> You will know it. Waves of relief and embarrassment, of elation and chagrin, are likely to sweep over you. Things that you have always known unconsciously about yourself will suddenly become clear, and life patterns will emerge. You can be sure that when this happens, you have identified your personality type correctly.[18]

As I said earlier, it may take some time to identify your preferred type, but once you do and are honest with yourself about it, you will know for sure.

One word of caution: As you read through the types, you will notice characteristics that seem just like someone you know—your spouse, your boss, your quirky uncle, your annoying neighbor. It's tempting to categorize people as a certain type through your own filter and knowledge of them. However, we can't really know the inner workings of a person. Many types appear similar on the outside, but the inner drive can be quite dissimilar. For instance, several people may show workaholic tendencies but are motivated by different strivings. One may think they should stay busy, another may be escaping boredom, one may be worried about their security, and another may be afraid of failing. Be careful about jumping to conclusions and labeling others. However, if you do recognize another person in the descriptions, let this bring a smile to your face and grace in your heart to see them in a new and liberating way. That is one of the great gifts of this typology—compassion and appreciation for the myriad of perspectives and gifts that make up humanity.

Before we embark on a tour of the types, I need to point out a few more components of the Enneagram structure. The following chapter explains how the types are divided into three triads, based on the three centers of human intelligence. You may also be wondering about the arrows on the drawing. These signify movements toward resourceful or non-resourceful living, an important consideration for personal growth. The meaning and value of the arrows will be addressed in the chapter following the descriptions of the nine types, along with two other elements called the Wings and Subtypes. Although these three elements may seem to make it complicated, once you grasp what they mean and how they work, they actually add more clarity and dynamism to the whole system.

6

THE CENTERS OF INTELLIGENCE

Remember the "programs for happiness" as Thomas Merton calls them—the strategies we've adopted to meet our primitive needs for survival and well-being—the needs for esteem and affection, safety and security, and power and control? These basic needs and strategies are represented on the Enneagram by three sections known as the "Centers." Included in each section are three of the personality types. The Centers are based on the primary sources of human intelligence: the heart, the head, and the body or gut. (We also have another transcendent spiritual intelligence I will discuss later.) Understanding these categories is helpful in recognizing the similarities of the three types in each group, as well as identifying how each type uses their preferred intelligence to meet their most basic needs.

We employ all three of these parts as humans. We feel, we think, and we act. When we are in a state of balance and integration (like a triangle), these sources of intelligence do their jobs appropriately and equally. For instance, when we need to make a decision, we can access all three centers to let us know what to choose. Our mind will collect data, sort through it, analyze and collate it, and come to a conclusion on what we "think" about the decision. Our heart will elicit emotions, tap into what we desire, consider the impact on our reputation and the effect on the lives of others, all leading us to know how we "feel" about the decision. Our body will have a gut response, reveal tension and tightness as we wrestle with what to do, and evoke a "sense" of the best course of action. With all centers working together, we can make an informed choice.

The problem is that we tend to rely on one of the Centers more than the other two. It will carry too much weight and influence. Generally, one of the other Centers will play a supporting or secondary role, and the third one is somewhat unavailable and repressed. In others words, we are usually out of balance when it comes to utilizing our sources of intelligence.

How does this apply? The nine types are divided up into these three groups. The Heart Types are Two, Three, and Four. The Head Types are Five, Six, and Seven. The Gut Types are Eight, Nine, and One. General characteristics of the particular Center are experienced similarly by each of the types in that Center. Also, each type in the Center expresses it differently.

The three Centers split the types like this:

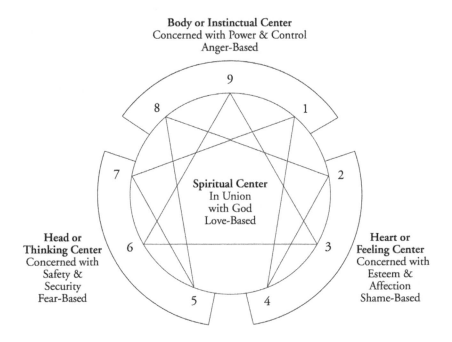

The Heart Center, sometimes called the Feeling Center, is the seat of our emotions and the ways we express them. It's our relational core that seeks to connect and belong with others. It's from here that we give and receive love, offer care and nurture, have empathy and compassion, create meaning about life, and express ourselves in artistic ways. In terms of the three basic human needs, those in the Heart Center are most concerned about establishing and maintaining esteem and affection. Their own self-image is a mirror on how others see them. Therefore, they focus on developing their public image so as to be noticed and accepted. Shame and sadness are common feelings for those in the Heart Center because they don't know if they are truly loved for who they are rather than what they do or how they appear. As we shall see, each of the Heart Types tries to earn esteem and affection in different ways. The Twos over-help, the Threes work to look successful, and the Fours strive to be seen as special.

The Head Center, sometimes called the Thinking Center, is the seat of our mental faculties. It's from here that we observe, analyze, conclude, categorize, remember, imagine, and plan. Our complex and active minds are filled with thoughts and ideas, all driven by the desire to make sense of the world. There is also wisdom and a way of knowing beyond the factual data. In terms of the three basic human needs, those in the Head Center are most concerned about their safety and security. They think things through to gain certainty and be prepared. Fear and anxiety are common for those in the Head Center because nothing is for sure and they are always aware of potential threats to their well-being. As we'll see, each of the Head Types approaches their need for safety and security differently. The Fives gather and analyze information, the Sixes prepare for the worst that could happen, and the Sevens plan ways to escape.

The Body or Gut Center, sometimes called the Instinctual Center, is the seat of our physical sensations, responses, and willfulness. It's from here that we react kinesthetically to our surroundings, like having a "gut sense" about something that has little to do with emotions or rationale. It's here that we feel energetic, passionate, engaged, and ready to move and get things done. In terms of the three basic needs, those in the Gut Center are most concerned with having power and maintaining control over both themselves and the world around them. They strive to establish independence, command respect, and resist whatever threatens their autonomy or tightly held convictions. Anger and rage are common reactions of those in the Gut Center. As we'll see, the three types in the Gut Center express their anger and their need for power and control in different ways. The Eights are intense and aggressive, the Nines are passive yet stubborn, and the Ones are judgmental and resentful.

What about the true Center of who we are—our spirit? First Corinthians 2:11 says, "For who knows a person's thoughts except their own spirit within them? In the same way no one knows the thoughts of God except the Spirit of God." Romans 8:16 indicates a link between our spirit and God's Spirit: "The Spirit himself testifies with our spirit that we are God's children." Several Scriptures differentiate between the soul and the spirit as two distinct aspects of our being. Many theologians define the "soul" as the combination of our emotions, mind, and will—our heart, head, and gut—and our "spirit" as the innermost part where God dwells, where we are in union with the divine, and where we spiritually discern the deeper truths of life. A thorough examination of this subject is beyond the scope of this book, but if we have a spiritual intelligence that is central to who we are, where might it be represented on the Enneagram picture? Remember that open space in the middle of the drawing? I remind you again of the powerful reality of being drawn toward the center where our spiritual knowing is connected and aligned with the love and presence of God's heart and mind. When we access our spiritual intelligence, then we can find true and lasting balance.

7 | THE NINE TYPES

"I believe that the Enneagram can help us find a deeper and more authentic relationship with God . . . it is not the answer, but one signpost among many. Signposts show the way, but we have to take the way ourselves."

—*Andreas Ebert,*
The Enneagram: A Christian Perspective

"Now the Lord is the Spirit, and where the Spirit of the Lord is, there is freedom. And we all, who with unveiled faces contemplate the Lord's glory, are being transformed into his image with ever-increasing glory, which comes from the Lord, who is the Spirit."
—*2 Corinthians 3:17-18*

As we start the tour of the nine types, please note how the descriptions of the personalities are organized. Each segment begins with two opposing quotes: one a Scripture related to God's character as reflected by the particular type and the other a quip that depicts the trap of the personality. The inherent genius of the type and the longing to experience and express the original connection to God's design are described in the opening paragraph.

Next you will read about the qualities of the Authentic Self, the *Wows* that show up when a person is at his or her best and living in what Richard Rohr calls a "redeemed" state.[19]

Manifestations of the Adapted Self, the *Eews*, follow, including some limitations and losses in childhood that may have been instrumental in forming the protective seed coat. I have intentionally exaggerated the negative, restrictive, and "unredeemed" characteristics here. This is where you can apply the "ugh test" to consider if this type might portray you. We all fall somewhere on a continuum between our best self and our worst self, so it's not an "either/or" kind of thing. Throughout this section, I've highlighted a few key elements of the type structure, including the distorted belief, the primary fear, the area of avoidance, and two other components that need further clarification: the focus of attention and the root sin or vice.

What is the focus of attention? It's what each personality concentrates on in order to maintain their protective strategy and persona. It's how their energy is directed internally and how this, in turn, affects their choices and actions. We can be so absorbed by one thing that we can't see anything else. Like blinders on a racehorse, the focus of attention eliminates distractions but also narrows the view, thereby missing the breadth of experience. Once we recognize our focus of attention and how it restricts us, we can shift it to something that is less confining. For instance, if I am focused on *what might go wrong* as I am walking down the street, my mental energy will be directed to thinking about any possibilities that might occur and how I will react to them. This creates anxiety and vigilance to watch for potential danger. Is that barking dog going to attack me? What will I do if I am mugged by the person walking toward me? Where could I hide if there was an earthquake? And so on. If I switch my focus to *trusting* I can handle whatever comes along, then my energy is directed to enjoying my walk and all the beauty around me, and I am more relaxed and open and able to embrace the present moment.

The root sin or vice is the primary emotional habit of each type. It is sometimes called "the passion." Remember, the nine sins or vices date back to the deadly sins identified by Ponticus Evagrius in early

Christianity, and *sin* is defined as "missing the true goal and scope of life." So each root sin should be considered in that context. It can be helpful to think of the word *vice* as a *vise* that squeezes you and holds you in place. This emotional habit is what holds each type in a constricted state. Included in the identification of the root sin for each type is how it influences a person's thoughts, feelings, and behaviors.

The final portion of the type descriptions is the exciting part—the Transformative Growth to Freedom. This describes the signs of new growth you might experience as the protective seed coat of your Adapted Self is disowned and released, and your Authentic Self is free to grow and flourish. These are indications of becoming more like Jesus as you follow on His path of letting go. These are not goals you set or improvements you determine to make. They are purely the work of God to transform you from the inside out as you are drawn toward the center and invited to live in the freedom and abundance of His Love.

Sprinkled throughout the type descriptions are reflections from people I've worked with and interviewed. Some stories are set apart and highlighted, while others flavored what I chose to emphasize. I am very grateful for the willingness of all those I interviewed to candidly share their life experiences with me and offer them to you. I hope their stories give you an understanding of how the various personality patterns impact and influence us in real, everyday life.

At the end of each type portrayal, I've provided a chart that summarizes the core elements as well as the redeemed and unredeemed characteristics of that type.

Also, a complete summary of all nine types is found on page 147.

Type One: A Reflection of God's Goodness and Rightness

*"Whatever is true, whatever is noble, whatever
is right, whatever is pure, whatever is lovely,
whatever is admirable—if anything is excellent or
praiseworthy, think about such things."*
—*Philippians 4:8*

*"Good, better, best—never let it rest,
Until the good gets better and the better gets best."*
—*Unknown*

Those who identify with Type One reflect God's perfection and righteousness and have a deep desire to experience the purity of the original human state—where all is good, complete, and unblemished. They possess an ideal vision for an ideal world in which all brokenness is healed and made whole again. The image of God imprinted on their very being is His goodness and holiness, and their deepest longing is to experience this and find expression for this divine gift in the world.

The following is a reflection offered by someone who identifies with the Type One pattern. Throughout all the type descriptions, you will see similar reflections from those I interviewed:

I yearn to connect and belong to something that is hugely Right, to be in the presence of and with Greatness, however it comes to me. When I gaze at the grandeur of mountains or listen to a musical masterpiece, my chest opens up and I stand taller. In moments like these, I feel the holy awe of bearing witness and being connected to Pure Magnificence and Perfection.

The Authentic Self

At their best, those with a Type One personality pattern are champions for excellence, live with integrity, and channel their energies into making the world a better place. They have an innate ability to see potential improvements and they bring their keen eye for detail to any endeavor in which they participate. They are responsible, trustworthy, conscientious, and highly principled. They work passionately for virtuous causes and commitments. Type Ones enjoy creating innovative ways to solve existing problems and they naturally know how to bring order out of chaos. Others are inspired by their lives to be and do their best for the good of all. Type Ones experience great satisfaction for a job well done and especially when their contribution is beneficial to others. A Type One individual said:

> In my work as a realtor, my team works hard to make improvements on a home to present it as perfectly as possible. We repair it, stage it, and present it in the best possible way. I love this about my job—it's such fun. The improvements are for everyone—the seller, the buyer, and even the neighborhood. Getting top dollar and my commission are just the exclamation points on the process for the betterment of everyone. It's an awesome moment to stand back and admire the finished product. It's tough to achieve because I will still see some flaws. But if I can allow for 95 percent perfection, it's amazing!

The Adapted Self

Because of their attunement to rightness and perfection, those who identify with Type One likely suffered deep disappointment and frustration early in life because nothing quite measured up to their desire for the ideal, including themselves. They wanted life to be orderly and predictable, but it just wasn't. When they were corrected as children, they interpreted it as a sign they were not good enough. It was painful for their shortcomings to be noticed. Although they often received praise for doing something well and had a pleasant feeling of satisfaction, this reinforced the perception they should do things perfectly. They learned to protect themselves from the shame of correction and punishment by being good and doing what was expected of them. Their early childhood experiences and their sensitivity to criticism contributed to the distorted belief that *"I am worthy of love and approval when I am perfect, good, and do what's right."*

This drive for perfection set in motion a life of re-creating rightness and goodness by reforming whatever seems flawed and incomplete. The original gift of God's perfection was skewed into a burden to make all things *right* in themselves, others, and the world. Their adaptive seed coat became an over-identification with their divine gift of goodness and they adopted the responsibility of being a standard-bearer for what "should be."

Thus for Type Ones, *the focus of attention is on what's wrong.* Their energy is directed toward criticizing or fixing whatever doesn't match their sense of rightness. They have high expectations and can be quite demanding. Because they are aware of so much that is wrong in the world and there is no end to what needs repair, they have difficulty relaxing. They pressure themselves, other people, and the groups they are associated with to improve and reach the ideal. For them, it is an endless cycle of noticing what's wrong, trying to reform it, and being frustrated and disappointed at their unmet standards of excellence.

Type Ones have an ever-present idea of what "perfect" might be and how impossible it is to attain it. They can quickly point out ways they fall short, like their messy closet or their 3.5 GPA. They resist being called a perfectionist because it's a deeper matter for them than having everything in order. Yet the standards are always there for them and their failures to measure up are evident to them more than to anyone else.

The root sin or vice for Type One is anger in the form of resentment. From their vantage point, nothing fully meets their longing for excellence and this is maddening. They resent the weight of responsibility to be in constant "reforming mode," especially when others don't seem to carry the same burden. This leaves little room for fun and frivolity as there is so much work to be done. Because it's not "right" to be angry, this resentment is generally below the surface and is experienced by others as a simmering and indignant presence. Most Ones are not aware of their anger and will shape their resentment into worthwhile activities, creating order, or suppressing their inner frustration. They tend to "harrumph" around, making their disapproval known without actually exploding or saying anything. However, those with whom they feel secure will often be targets of this contained resentment.

The anger of Ones also takes the form of judgment, both toward themselves and others. Their own relentless inner critic is like a judge following them around and reminding them of how they messed up or could be better. Deep within, this judgment taps into *their primary fear of being unworthy of love and grace because of their imperfections.* The associated guilt motivates them to quiet this inner critic by being vigilant to *avoid making mistakes.* But the judge rarely lets up, leaving them tired, tense, and on guard against any kind of criticism. Another Type One said:

> I put a lot of energy into making something perfect and to avoid any failing. I will work tirelessly on an event to ensure that it goes off without a hitch. However, I assume it will only get done right if I do it, and I spend sleepless nights reviewing all the details so it will live up to my standards. I'm furious when others don't do their part. Being disappointed in some small detail of the event will spoil it for me. I can receive all the accolades for a job well done but will obsess over what went wrong and will quickly write a list of needed improvements for next time. Anything that wasn't perfect becomes a judgment on myself that I missed it.

This inner critic also spills over into how they view and accept others, which, in turn, impacts their relationships. Because Ones categorize things in life as right or wrong, good or bad, perfect or imperfect, godly or evil, they tend to either correct or reject whatever or whoever doesn't fit the right side of the scale as they see it. They encourage people to better themselves but aren't aware that these self-improvement plans for others are not always welcomed. For them, it's an act of love to make suggestions. After all, who doesn't want to be the best they can be? Why would someone not want to make positive changes in their life? From the One standpoint, they are doing someone a great favor by pointing out ways to improve. But the recipient can sense the lack of acceptance and approval, and the suggestions can feel more like condemnation. This can be a source of strain in relationships.

> Everything I have approached in life is from the standpoint of reforming everything, including myself and other people. I see things as they could be. It's a curse—the ability to see things that are wrong and feel the burden to correct them. For instance, when I was in church leadership, I saw inconsistencies in the system and would pull people together to address it and fix it. Unfortunately, this created a lot of pain and agony for others and for me. In my professional work, this reforming ability is useful, but not always in other arenas, like my family life and personal relationships.

Type Ones are located in the Gut Center on the Enneagram. Their experience of imperfection is visceral and demands a response. Their intuitive awareness of problems, those in their own life or globally, is painful and they are compelled to offer potential solutions where they can make a difference. Even simple things, like a picture askew or disorderly surroundings, bother them physically. Like the other Gut types, they also have a high need for power and control. They address this by a constant vigilance over their environment, work, people, and themselves so there will be no slippery slope into imperfection and a compromise of standards. Everything may not be in order in their life, but the reality of this is a cause of inner distress. Their endless efforts to bring about the perfection that only God can creates tension throughout their bodies.

All Ones I have talked with say that experiencing the pure beauty and wildness of nature is deeply moving for them. Their hearts soar and their whole being relaxes. They don't have to fix anything because it's perfect just as it is. They can simply breathe in the majesty of creation—the rolling hills of wheat, a sunset over the ocean, or watching someone pull in a fish. The rawness feeds something deep in their soul and they feel a connection with holy rightness. These moments may be fleeting, but they call them back to their divine gift and longing for the perfection and completeness of God.

Transformative Growth to Freedom

If a person identifies with the personality patterns of Type One, what qualities of their Authentic Self will emerge as they disown and soften the protective seed coat of their Adapted Self? How will they become more like Jesus as they follow Him? Here's a perspective of a Type One:

> As I am growing into more freedom in Christ, I realize that I don't always have to be right. I can accept others and the choices they make without feeling the compulsion to correct or challenge them. I can accept my shortcomings and mistakes with more grace. This is a more open and settled place for me, and it feels like true wisdom.

Type Ones will experience more serenity, patience, and joy as they release their "should monitor" and their need to be right and perfect. They will come to know they are worthy just because they *are* and can be set free from trying to earn their value. An internal spaciousness will open them to God's unmerited grace and love. By trusting God as the true source and author of perfection and completeness, Ones can let go of their identity as a moral compass. A new sense of ease and acceptance will replace the constant burden to reform and control.

For Ones, shifting the focus of attention from noticing what is wrong to celebrating what is right and good is a relief. When they release resentments and extend forgiveness, their hearts become more gracious, loving, and appreciative. Accepting that everyone is responsible for their own growth allows room for more patience with shortcomings and mistakes. They are more lighthearted and spontaneous. In a new space of freedom to live as their Authentic Self, God's true perfection and goodness will flow through them, and their endeavors to bring wholeness and healing in the world will be fruitful and lasting, but without the underlying strife and pressure of their Adapted Self pattern of needing to right every wrong.

TYPE ONE

Divine Gift:	God's goodness and rightness
Core Need:	To be right and perfect
Focus of Attention:	What's wrong and needs correction
Root Sin:	Resentment
Avoidance:	Making mistakes and being criticized
Primary Fear:	Being unworthy
Transformational Growth:	Grace and patience

Authentic Self	Adapted Self
Redeemed Qualities	**Unredeemed Characteristics**
Principled	Perfectionistic
Noble	Judgmental
Conscientious	Rigid
Responsible	Obstinate
Idealistic	Intolerant
Ethical	Dogmatic
Hardworking	Critical of others
Persevering	Overly serious
Thorough	Abrasive
Strives for excellence	Demanding
Works for good of all	Uptight

Type Two: A Reflection of God's Love and Care

"This is how we know what love is: Jesus Christ laid down his life for us. And we ought to lay down our lives for our brothers and sisters. If anyone has material possessions and sees a brother or sister in need but has no pity on them, how can the love of God be in that person? Dear children, let us not love with words or speech but with actions and in truth."

—*1 John 3:16-18*

"The most painful thing is losing yourself in the process of loving someone too much, and forgetting that you are special too."

—*Ernest Hemingway*

Those who identify with Type Two reflect God's unconditional and unlimited love and nurture for all people. They are naturally in tune with the needs of others and desire to be a conduit of God's abundant love to a hurting world. The imprinted image of God on their very being is for all hearts to be connected and for all needs to be met. They long to experience the unconditional love of God for themselves and to express the fullness of His love and care in tangible ways. A Type Two said:

> When I see love in action, my endorphins just pop. I feel like my whole bloodstream is flooded with trueness, peace, and balance. I like to look out in the world and see the way people love—it captures me and is very fulfilling to think about the power of love in the world.

The Authentic Self

At their best, those with a Type Two personality pattern are open-hearted, charming, supportive, and genuinely interested in other people. Life for them is about relational connections and they enjoy many treasured friendships. Their mission is to make the world a more loving and caring place. Twos have a sixth sense for what other people need and delight in meeting those needs. Hospitality is their middle name and everyone around them feels welcomed and special. They will stand by others in their time of greatest difficulties and be the first to offer practical support. They are empathic and sensitive to the feelings of others. When someone hurts, they hurt; when someone is joyful, they share their joy. Twos can be benevolent and generous with their time, talent, and resources to care for the welfare of others without expecting anything in return. They also inspire others to do the same so everyone will know they are loved, provided for, and valued. Individuals who identify with Type Two expressed it this way:

> It is deeply satisfying for me when I rally the troops to care for someone who is hurting or sick. When my father was ill, I organized all of the family members to be sure that he and my mom were not alone and that their practical needs were taken care of. When my orchestration worked, I felt light and joyful that we lessened their burden and pain. I was like a bulldog to make sure it happened and it was worth it.

> If someone hasn't been loved, I just want show them that they are loved. Seeing someone thrive just delights my heart—there is a lot of joy there for me. I realize that my life's purpose is to let God pour His grace and unconditional love on me, and it will overflow to whomever God brings into my life. I will stay with people through thick and thin. I want them to know the endless love of God.

The Adapted Self

Because of their attunement to love and nurture, those who identify with Type Two likely perceived a withdrawal of love and approval early in life when they were scolded for not being kind or considerate of others. At the same time, they were applauded for sharing, acting unselfishly, and being helpful, all of which came quite naturally to them. On one hand, they felt shamed for their apparent selfishness, and on the other, they felt affirmed for their loving nature. They learned to guard their tender hearts from the distress of shame by connecting with others and earning love by taking care of them. These early experiences and their attunement to God's love contributed to the distorted belief that *"I am loved and esteemed if I care for others without regard for my own needs."* Constructing their lives around this lie is a source of suffering for Twos.

As a result, Type Twos expend their energy attempting to re-create God's love and nurture by giving selflessly without boundaries and by dismissing their own needs as irrelevant. They take the words of Jesus that "it is better to give than to receive" to a new level of self-sacrifice and denial. Deep down, they experience a sadness that they are unlovable as they are and believe they will be rejected or disliked if they fail to attend to the needs of others. This is a place of suffering for them. The protective seed coat for Twos is an over-identification with their divine gift of love and nurture and feeling the burden to "make love happen" by their own resources.

Thus for Type Twos, *the focus of attention is on the needs of others.* They scan the social horizon for how they can help and when they see a need, they sense an urgency to step in even if it's not requested of them. Sometimes they assume needs that aren't even there. They believe they must help in order to stay connected with others and maintain an admirable standing in their community. In a way, they seduce others into needing them, and this can seem manipulative, intrusive, and overbearing. When they aren't needed, they feel disconnected from people and will go into overdrive to figure out a way to contribute and help.

As part of the Heart Center, Type Twos are concerned with their public image and they have a high need for esteem and affection. So they seek validation by being needed and indispensable. They tend to talk about ways they have helped and look for attention and appreciation for their thoughtful service. They want to be known as the ultimate givers, even to the point of being martyrs and rescuers. Even God must be impressed with how they serve sacrificially and without limits. Though they find joy in giving, they are apt to over-give, often to a point of exhaustion. If their help is not acknowledged, they feel hurt and slighted. This may be harbored as underlying bitterness or expressed in verbal accusations of being taken for granted or ignored. Since they rely on the approval of others for their unselfish giving, *the primary fear for Type Twos is being useless and unable to help.*

> I have a hard time saying No. I get myself in situations I wish I wouldn't have and then I stress about how to get out of them. It can be overwhelming since there are so many people who could use my help and I don't want to disappoint them. I know in my head that I can't meet all needs, but my emotions never catch up to that.

The root sin or vice for Type Twos is pride. This shows up in two ways. The first is the belief that they know how best to meet someone's needs, even better than the one who appears to need their help. This is a "messiah complex" of sorts. They take pride in their astute ability to take care of people and situations, and they wear a badge of honor for the help and advice they generously give. Their over-involvement in people's lives can feel patronizing and communicates that the other is incapable of taking care of their own needs without the Two's intervention. This reinforces their skewed need to be needed.

Another manifestation of the sin of pride is the *avoidance of their own needs and wants.* They turn away from themselves in order to turn toward others. It feels selfish and wrong to care for themselves as this goes against their identity as the one who helps. The details of their personal lives are often in chaos because they are easily pulled away to give their time and energy for others. They have a hard time asking for help and will divert attention away from their own neediness. They don't want to be dependent on others or a burden to them. When people do help, they feel guilty and obligated to repay them rather than simply receiving and being grateful. These forms of pride are summed up in the unbalanced foundation of many of their relationships: "After all I have done for you, you owe me your friendship, admiration, and gratitude."

Transformative Growth to Freedom

If a person identifies with the personality patterns of Type Two, what qualities of their Authentic Self will emerge as they disown and soften the protective seed coat of their Adapted Self? How will they become more like Jesus as they follow Him?

> My first reaction in situations of need is that I should be the one to help or do something. I am learning to ask the Lord if this is where He is calling me to help before I jump in without pausing. This is a place of discernment for me—to recognize that God has a part for me to play, but I don't need to carry all the burdens and brokenness of the world.

> I lived for a long time with a "love pit" where hurts lived and I earned love by a dysfunctional imbalance of attention on others. I really feel this pit when there is a loss of connection with someone. This love pit isn't so deep when I am connected to love from God and love for myself. I try to turn to Him for love rather than looking to others for it.

Type Twos will experience more humility, pure love, and true generosity when they surrender their habitual need to be needed. They are able to receive love from God and others without trying to earn it by over-helping. Humility means admitting their own needs and making room for personal care in their busy lives without feeling guilty. In the process of restoration to their Authentic Self, Twos sense a deep repentance when they recognize that much of their giving has been motivated by their own subconscious needs for love and esteem. This is just the opposite of how they see themselves. It is through this honest humiliation that they can relax their compulsion to help whenever they see a need. They gain liberty to say no and to accept that their assistance is not always appropriate or wanted. This sets others free to help themselves and not need them so much. As a result, others feel more at ease around them. The pure love that emerges is unconditional and without any strings attached.

A Two who has shifted his or her focus of attention from the needs of others to a trust in God's love apart from their giving will become a wise and discerning servant, depending and trusting that He will direct them to help others if and when He needs their particular gifts of service and nurture. True and genuine love will flow from them without a demand for affirmation or reciprocity, and they will enjoy more mutuality in relationships as they graciously accept love and help from others.

TYPE TWO

Divine Gift:	God's unconditional love and care
Core Need:	To be needed
Focus of Attention:	The needs of others
Root Sin:	Pride
Avoidance:	Their own needs and desires
Primary Fear:	Being useless
Transformational Growth:	Humility and pure love

Authentic Self	Adapted Self
Redeemed Qualities	**Unredeemed Characteristics**
Nurturing	Possessive
Generous	Intrusive
Attentive	Flatterer
Compassionate	Manipulative
Hospitable	Possessive
Sensitive	Effusive
Unselfish	Overly accommodating
Benevolent	Martyr-like
Affirming	Seeks appreciation
Supportive	Patronizing
Openhearted	Indispensable

Type Three: A Reflection of God's Hope and Radiance

"Record the vision and inscribe it on tablets, that the one who reads it may run. For the vision is yet for the appointed time; it hastens toward the goal and it will not fail. Though it tarries, wait for it; for it will certainly come, it will not delay."
—*Habakkuk 2:2-3 NASB*

"There is no such thing as failure. There are only results."
—*Tony Robbins*

Those who identify with Type Three reflect God's vision for a glorious future—for themselves, for others, and for the world. They emanate hope. Threes desire to experience the radiance of the original human state—where all shine in the kingdom of God. They believe everyone has a unique genius and a significant part to play in the unfolding of something great. The image of God imprinted on their very being is unwavering hope and radiance. Their deepest longing is to experience their own brilliance as a child of God and to find expression for the divine gift of hope in the world. A Type Three individual shared:

> I feel overcome with emotion and inspiration when I witness ordinary people doing extraordinary things; my heart is filled with awe when they break through barriers and accomplish more than they dreamed possible. It is even more thrilling when I can be a part of drawing out their greatness and opening up new possibilities of hope for their lives.

The Authentic Self

At their best, those with a Type Three personality pattern are optimistic about the future, effective leaders, get things done with competence and excellence, and bring out the best in people. They can imagine "what could be" in any personal or collective story. They inspire people to dream together, set goals, and implement steps to fulfill whatever they set out to do. Threes can envision the positive results of an endeavor before it has even begun. They speak about it with confidence and mobilize everyone else to believe in it too. They enjoy forward progress and the effects of their dedication and hard work. Threes are admired for their many accomplishments and talents, many of which bring hope and advancement in the world. One of their greatest strengths is seeing the inherent potential in others and encouraging the expression of their genius.

> My heart sings when the synergy of a well-functioning and affirming team realizes a worthy goal together. It happens when people's gifts are maximized, everyone makes their unique contribution, and what we accomplish together is more than we ever could have alone. Life, for me, is a team sport and I love to celebrate success with others.

> It's a wonderful feeling of satisfaction when a project is going really well and when the task is finally complete and everything I worked so hard to manage plays out as I had hoped . . . or was even better than I expected. Chasing that emotional high is worth all of the self-denial, long hours, and hard work just to feel for a few minutes the gratification of a task well done. I don't enjoy it for too long because there is always something new and exciting on the horizon.

The Adapted Self

Early in life, those with a Type Three propensity likely experienced shame and embarrassment for not performing well in the eyes of others. They also received attention and praise for their achievements and leadership abilities. They interpreted their successes as markers of their value, rather than knowing their intrinsic worth apart from them. Failure was painful, especially if they perceived a loss of affection from those important to them. They learned to protect their tender hearts by being competitive and working harder than anyone else to come out on top. Over time, they came to believe that *"I am loved and respected if I perform well and accomplish much."* Constructing their lives around this lie is a source of suffering for Threes.

This drive to portray an image of success set in motion a life of trying to establish their own worth and brilliance by productivity, achievement, and an impressive public image. As with the other types in the Heart Center, they care deeply what others think of them. Because of this, they over-identify with their performance; their external persona defines and motivates them. They set high goals for themselves. They avoid failure and looking incompetent. Type Threes have an innate sense of what might look successful and the role they need to play in any given situation and they figure out how to perform it. If humor is expected, they will be funny. If deep conversations are required, they will engage in provocative interactions. If their goals or roles are unclear, they feel at a loss. Negative feedback is unsettling and they will work to overcome a bad report. With their protective seed coat intact, they send out commercials for themselves to gain recognition and admiration, and they boast about their projects, successes, and connections to ensure the high regard of others. Type Threes live with an underlying sadness that they are loved for what they achieve rather than for who they really are on the inside.

Thus for Type Threes, *the focus of attention is on tasks and goals.* Their energy goes to getting things done and they organize life around the endless list of things they want to make happen. This list rarely gets shorter. Because they innately intuit the actions needed to ensure desired results, they carry the weight of responsibility for driving a project forward. Once a goal is met, they add something new that captures their attention. Their divine gift of hope can be skewed into creating a future that supports their own need to appear successful. While their energy is directed toward the future, they can miss what is present to them in the here and now. The tyranny of tasks and goals often preempts attention to their personal life and relationships. Because their self-esteem is attached to what they accomplish, their *primary fear is being incapacitated and unable to perform well.* Here's an example of Type Three thinking:

> I experience "task-tension" to get things done, to progress, to be on top of things, and to check things off my list. The drive is all internal and I have felt a lot of pressure to be continually achieving and accomplishing. There is a side to this that I love and it energizes me. And it can also be burdensome and overwhelming.

Because of their drive to get things done, Type Threes can be out of touch with their own feelings. For them, emotions are counterproductive and often get in the way of progress. It doesn't matter if they are afraid, sad, or angry as long as the job gets done. Even though they are in the Heart Center, they do not access this part of themselves very easily or comfortably. Their drive for success is at the expense of being connected to their inner self.

> It's lonely sometimes to be so focused and I tend to isolate myself when I am stressed. Over the years I have lost track of who I really am inside. I was just whoever the church or my job needed me to be. I am starting to pick up the threads of myself now and to realize I am more than what I look like on the outside.

When Threes define themselves by their accomplishments, they can use people as a means to their own end. They genuinely care about people and enjoy many relationships but don't often set aside time or energy to invest in those who aren't in their immediate scope of action. If someone is moving in the same direction as a Three, he or she will be valued and included. If they are not or once a goal has been reached, intentional investment in the relationship often disappears.

The root sins or vices for Type Three are deceit and vainglory. They know how to put a positive spin on anything. Deceit does not necessarily manifest in bold-faced lies, but in subtle distortions to make themselves and their endeavors look successful. The place of greatest deception is with themselves. They have a hard time admitting their limitations and failures because it goes against their identity as someone who is competent and able to accomplish anything they set out to do. If something appears to be headed for failure, they will blame others for not doing their part or they will abandon it altogether in order to save face. Vainglory means their external persona is more important than their internal world. They stand outside themselves and watch how they perform, measuring their value by standards of success. Rather than believing their true identity as a child of God apart from what they do, they believe the lie "I am what I do."

Transformative Growth to Freedom

If a person identifies with the personality patterns of Type Three, what qualities of their Authentic Self will emerge as they disown and soften the protective seed coat of their Adapted Self? How will they become more like Jesus as they follow Him? One Type Three shared these thoughts:

> In my new work, I leverage my Three-ness as a way of creating progress for other people. It is not about me but about the results

for them. It is very satisfying to help them grow and accomplish something great. I am not so focused on my own success, but on the success of others. I resonate with Jesus' words to Peter to feed His lambs. This is my calling right now and I really love it.

Type Threes will become more truthful, relaxed, and trusting as they release their need to appear successful. Their gift of true hope will break through their fears and relieve the pressure to get things done. They will seek to be led by God to put their gifts of leadership and vision into action without relying on them for their identity. They will access their own heart and become more honest with themselves and others about their feelings, limitations, and failings. They will relax and trust that God will unfold the future as He desires and that it's not their sole responsibility to make something happen. They can hold their accomplishments loosely and be humbly grateful for the ways God uses them to further His purposes rather than for their own public image. They stick with endeavors even though there is a hint of potential failure.

A Three who has shifted his or her focus of attention and energy from their tasks and goals will be able to embrace a vision larger than their current ambition. They will realize that most of their objectives will be accomplished, but without the worry and drive that keep them from focusing on other things. They will be more faithful in nurturing their relationships and will care for people apart from the contribution they make. They will be able to put time and effort into their own personal growth and enjoyment without anxiety about ground that may be lost if they do.

TYPE THREE

Divine Gift:	Hope and radiance
Core Need:	To appear successful
Focus of Attention:	Tasks and goals
Root Sin:	Deceit and vainglory
Avoidance:	Failure and incompetence
Primary Fear:	Being incapacitated
Transformational Growth:	Truthfulness and trust

Authentic Self	Adapted Self
Redeemed Qualities	Unredeemed Characteristics
Productive	Image-conscious
Energetic	Insensitive
Empowering	Exploitative
Visionary	Defensive
Focused	Workaholic
Hardworking	Expedient
Optimistic	Superficial
Team builder	Self-promoting
Competent	Success-driven
Goal-oriented	Arrogant
Motivating	Self-deceptive

Type Four: A Reflection of God's Creativity and Depth

"I will give thanks to You, for I am fearfully and wonderfully made.
Wonderful are Your works; my soul knows it very well.
My frame was not hidden from You, when I was being made in secret,
and skillfully wrought in the depths of the earth."

—*Psalm 139:14-15 NASB*

"He who is not contented with what he has
would not be contented with what he would like to have."

—*Socrates*

Those who identify with Type Four reflect God's beauty and originality as expressed through the uniqueness of every created being and every sacred moment of life. They desire to experience the pure human state—where all is authentic, exquisite, and enough. They draw from the deep well of God's creativity to bring forth His unfathomable riches for all to encounter. Their deep longing is to experience and express their intimate connection to the depth and beauty of God. A Type Four expressed it this way:

> I feel most alive when I am surrounded by the beauty of creation, both in nature and in people. I feel a generosity in my own spirit when I am in a deep conversation with someone who allows me a sacred entrance into their inner life. When I am immersed in creativity, I feel my insides relax like an iron gate is pulled open in me. My guard goes down and grace shows up.

The Authentic Self

At their best, those with a Type Four pattern are intuitive, imaginative, and inspire others to notice deep meaning in the simplest of things. For them, everyone and everything is sacred and special. Life is about the rich inner journey and bringing forth one's extraordinary self. Because a wide range of emotions are available to them, they are sensitive to the moods and feelings of others and are able to empathize with them. Fours have an artistic flair that is expressed in their own individual way, such as how they dress, their metaphoric language, their decorating style, or their creative pursuits. The possibilities are as original as they are. They have an antenna for what is sincere and real. Their intensity and appreciation for life spills over and enriches their relationships, faith, work, and artistic callings. They are romantic and refined. They endeavor to express their connection with the depth and beauty of life in meaningful ways, even though it pains them to realize they can never adequately express this so others experience it in the same way.

> My intense feelings are physical and beautiful. I feel them throughout my body. When it's sunny outside, I feel teary at the beauty and warmth. When I see children playing, my heart fills with joy. When I see flowers dying, I grieve their loss. As a child, I would be sad at dusk because the day was ending and gone forever. My amplified emotions are very real and authentic in the moment, even if they don't make sense to anyone else.

The Adapted Self

Because of their attunement to emotional connection and uniqueness, those who identify with Type Four likely suffered a sense of rejection and abandonment when they realized they were either just one of the crowd or were on the outside looking in. By blending in or feeling left out, they wondered why they were not special enough to be noticed. They perceived that something was missing in them or they had a deep flaw that made them unremarkable. On the other hand, they were singled out for their artistry or received attention for ways they were different, like their offbeat sense of humor. Being noticed became important to their sense of self. Because they experienced and expressed a breadth of emotions, they often felt shame for being too much, misunderstood, or different. They learned to protect their tender hearts by standing out in some way or creating a world of fantasy within themselves. These early childhood experiences and their sensitivity to the extraordinariness of each person led them to believe that *"I need to be special to be noticed and wanted, and something is wrong with me."* Constructing their lives around this lie is a source of suffering for Fours.

> I grew up in a rather rigid environment where my imagination was not valued or encouraged. So as a means of survival, I created a world of stories within myself. For instance, when I had to practice the piano, I envisioned a story of myself twirling or flying or playing with the music as a background to my fantasy.

> When someone asked me why I was crying at my sixth birthday party, I said, "because I'm leaving the best five years of my life behind."

Their original connection to the beauty and originality of life was distorted into a drive to re-create their own uniqueness and express it in original ways that will be noticed. Their adaptive seed coat became an over-identification with the qualities and talents that made them unique. Thus Fours overdo being special. They avoid being ordinary or blending in. They feel a sense of panic that they will disappear if they are just like everyone else. Type Fours will even sabotage their own lives in order to maintain their individuality. While they are trying to be special, they also feel left out and different. They believe that no one could ever grasp the depths of their internal world and they *deeply fear being a nobody who is misunderstood, unknown, and alone.*

Thus for Type Fours, *the focus of attention is on what's missing.* They have an "if only . . . " view of life. They fantasize about a time when they will finally have what will satisfy all of their longings, like an ideal soul mate, a future experience, aesthetic surroundings, or the realization of an unfulfilled dream. They also reminisce about the past, either with sweet nostalgia, loss, or painful regret. They ponder how their deficiencies keep them from being enough. All these ways of focusing their attention toward what is missing makes them discontent with the present and unappreciative of what they do have. The missing link to their happiness always seems just out of reach. A Type Four reflected:

> What shows up for me is a sense of regret for what I missed in my life by the choices I made. It's not so much about what is missing now, but what could have been. My emotional memory holds on to these dashed hopes. I feel mad at God because I think I missed things He could have made sure I didn't. This makes it hard for me to accept my life and enjoy what I have.

The root sin or vice for Type Four is envy. They look at the lives of others who seem to have a more fulfilling life and long for what they have. This is a dilemma for them: they desire to be their own unique person, yet they also measure themselves against others who seem to have more class, more love, more talent, more significance. This can lead to hostility or to a deep sadness that they will never have what will make them complete.

> Life feels like a zero-sum game. When I compare myself with others, I exaggerate their gifts and minimize mine. Who they are and what they do takes something away from me, so I can't celebrate them. I have a hard time valuing myself because I see what I'm not in comparison to other people. Someone else is always better than me and has more of what I want.

Because of their longing for authenticity and sincerity, Type Fours are compelled to express their ever-changing emotions in words, actions, or creative outlets. One moment they exude happiness and the next moment they are sad and blue. The expression of their inner emotional life can be flamboyant or subtle, and there is often a sweet sadness about them. This may seem dramatic and moody to others, but it feels real and essential to them. To be otherwise feels insincere and boring. It is hard for them to recognize how this unbridled drive for expression can actually prevent them from getting what they really want.

> I bring on my biggest fear of not being heard when I am overdramatic to get my point across. I sabotage myself. If I can tame my emotions and still express my opinion, things always work out better. This takes a lot of effort on my part because it's so unnatural.

Type Fours are easily bored with ordinary routines and disdain whatever seems mundane. They will manufacture emotional intensity just to stir life up and make it more dramatic. They are prone to exaggeration and will fabricate stories that go beyond the basic facts to make things more captivating. Along this same line, Type Fours will create a story about the motivation and meaning of what others say and do, especially as it relates to them.

Like Type Twos and Threes in the Heart Center, Type Fours see themselves through the eyes of others and long to be deeply connected in relationships. They want to portray an image of being unlike anyone else, standing out as matchless and distinguished from all others. They value relationships where they connect deeply at the heart. Their natural instinct for empathy can be overwhelming as they absorb the sufferings of others. Fours often create "push-pull" relationships in which they pull people to them and then push them away so they can long for them again. It is also how they test if the other person will really stay. This can lead them to feel dissatisfied in relationships because they never quite measure up to the intense emotional bond that seems more real and honest. They don't understand that not everyone can meet them there.

Transformative Growth to Freedom

If a person identifies with the personality patterns of Type Four, what qualities of their Authentic Self will emerge as they disown and soften the protective seed coat of their Adapted Self? How will they become more like Jesus as they follow Him? A Type Four said:

> I am learning to realize that everyone has an ordinary life just like mine rather than romanticizing that others have a more satisfying life. I am learning that I can make my own everyday life extraordinary by enjoying simple things around me and adding touches that make them special to me. It doesn't have to be a whole new experience for me to be happy.

Type Fours will experience more contentment, equanimity, and gratitude as they release their need to be unique and special. They will learn to embrace their emotional swings with love and acceptance and be grateful for the depth of feelings they experience more than other people. When they are centered on God's completeness, they will cease longing to be completed by something beyond their reach. As they accept their own gifts, they will also find themselves more open and appreciative of the gifts of others without be threatened or diminished. They will become more realistic about life and embrace the beauty of its ordinariness.

When they shift their focus from what's missing, they will recognize they have all they need to be fulfilled and happy rather than longing for something more. A new contentment and peace will settle within them, allowing them to enjoy the sacredness of each moment without needing to create a dramatic experience. They will grow in empathy with other people without bearing their suffering for longer than they need to. With the freedom of Jesus, they will come to see the beauty of their individuality and will know deep within that they are special just because they are His.

TYPE FOUR

Divine Gift:	God's creativity and depth
Core Need:	To be special
Focus of Attention:	What's missing
Root Sin:	Envy
Avoidance:	Ordinariness and blending in
Primary Fear:	Being unnoticed
Transformational Growth:	Contentment and gratitude

Authentic Self	Adapted Self
Redeemed Qualities	**Unredeemed Characteristics**
Authentic	Moody
Creative	Withdrawn
Sensitive	Impractical
Compassionate	Depressive
Perceptive	Self-absorbed
Intuitive	Melancholic
Refined	Dramatic
Sincere	Possessive
Sentimental	Eccentric
Original	Self-pitying
Expressive	Exaggerated

Type Five: A Reflection of God's Wisdom and Truth

"For the Lord gives wisdom;
from his mouth come knowledge and understanding. . . .
For wisdom will enter your heart,
and knowledge will be pleasant to your soul.
Discretion will protect you, and understanding will guard you."
—*Proverbs 2:6, 10-11*

"You are either withholding your love in fear or
giving your deepest gifts."
David Deida

Those who identify with Type Five reflect God's wisdom and a deep inner knowing that illuminates the mind and heart. They are keen observers who are able to bring forth simplicity in the midst of life's complexities. When they experience moments of clear understanding, they sense a holy awe at belonging to profound truth. As one who is connected to the wisdom of God, they long to comprehend the deeper realities of life and apply this knowledge for the sake of living well in the world. A Type Five individual said:

> When I discover a new piece of interesting information, it's like the sensation of eating the best delicacies. Or when I connect the dots and realize a new insight, it's like the "Hallelujah Chorus" goes off inside me. And I love to pass it along so others will discover and connect with the same understanding. I find this deeply gratifying and almost intoxicating.

The Authentic Self

At their best, those with a Type Five personality pattern are inquis-itive, innovative, and insightful. They are masters at condensing a wide scope of data into simple, practical information for others to grasp and use. It's a wonder to behold when they articulate the gist of a complicated subject in a few clarifying statements. As perceptive observers, they delight in noticing precise details and discovering interesting facts that others might miss. They like to collect and analyze information so they can make educated decisions. Type Fives are often experts in a chosen field of knowledge and investigate every possible thing to know about it. It's satisfying enough if they are interested in the subject matter, but it's a bonus if it makes a contribution to the world. Many Type Fives are teachers who enjoy enlightening others. They have a rational approach to life that helps people consider various viewpoints on complex issues. Fives can remain objective in emotional or chaotic situations, bringing a sense of calm and reason. They enjoy working alone and periods of privacy anchor them in the midst of demands for their time and energy. Type Fives are logical and grounded, and gifted at unpacking puzzling situations until a right answer comes together. Their brilliant minds and practical application of knowledge combine to supply useful wisdom for themselves and others.

> When I am coaching customers, it is deeply fulfilling to provide them with insights and common sense so they can make an informed decision to resolve their personal issues. It feels good to share my expertise so they understand all of their possible choices and ramifications. I enjoy the positive feedback loop when I see them apply my information and make a logical choice that benefits them.

The Adapted Self

Because of their attunement to wisdom and inner knowing, those who identify with Type Five likely felt foolish and caught off guard when they didn't know enough about something in their early life. When they drew a blank, they felt stupid and embarrassed, causing a sense of insecurity and emptiness. Most Type Fives are introverted, and this may have been a source of discomfort as they tried to manage their energy in a demanding environment. They often preferred to just let life go by without engaging too much. They perceived themselves as lacking important information to make sense of their world, yet gained social status for their astute minds, ease of learning, and ability to grasp complex ideas. They learned to survive in a world that required too much of them by withdrawing into the safe haven of their minds. These types of early childhood experiences contributed to the false belief that *"I will be safe and self-sufficient if I am perceptive and well-informed."* Constructing their lives around this lie is a source of suffering for Fives. A Type Five put it this way:

> When I think of my childhood, I don't recall much interaction directed toward me. I assumed I was loved, but I didn't ask for much attention. I spent a lot of time reading and playing by myself. I remember I would crawl behind the couch with a little light so I could be alone to read. I was content to do this for hours.

Type Fives are motivated to gather enough information to fill up an inner emptiness and a perceived shortage of resources to face what is demanded of them. Life, for them, often seems like too much to handle and they withdraw into their own private world of thoughts and concepts to escape. They resist intrusions into their personal space and need time to re-engage if necessary. The protective seed coat for Type Fives is an over-identification with their divine gift of wisdom as they try to re-create an "inner knowing" by studying and synthesizing. This need to perceive and know compels them to diligently search for the keys that will unlock some truth and give them a sense of competence and assurance.

Although I am a social person, my entire life is filtered through my head. I am constantly bouncing ideas off myself; my mind is my greatest ally and sometimes my greatest enemy. When I am with friends, I constantly try to find out information about them. If I am in a large group, I pay close attention to all the interactions and assess the feelings of the room and the tone of everyone in it. Then I will go home and replay all of my interactions to see if there is any useful info I need to retain. Thinking is my main mode of operation.

Thus for Type Fives, *the focus of attention is on figuring out what makes sense.* They concentrate their energy on research, analysis, and drawing conclusions about what is true based on their findings. Once they understand something, they feel secure and satisfied. This means they may ruminate about an unsettled question for a long time. Once they are certain about something, they can become attached to their reasoned ideas and will resist being challenged to think otherwise. They dislike being considered incorrect. Since there is so much data to process, they will sort and compartmentalize everything into smaller segments to bring order to their overactive minds. This is helpful to a point, but the tendency to fit all aspects of life into categories leaves little room for nuance and mystery.

Yet they can be quite mysterious, eccentric, and reclusive. They retreat and ruminate over abstract ideas and concepts, distancing themselves from the practical realities of life. Their eccentricity shows up in their quirky sense of humor, investigation of unusual topics, creative imagination, and "out of the box" views. Also, because of their breadth of knowledge, they can set themselves apart as intellectually superior, to the point of being cynical and contemptuous of those who are less informed.

Type Fives are collectors. They not only gather information but also whatever holds special interest for them, like books, historical artifacts, educational materials, personal letters, newspaper articles, and other pieces of interesting informaton. In some way, this fills up their inner void. They often have file boxes crammed with papers that once supplied valuable information for them. They hang onto these just in case they may need them someday. This penchant for collecting creates a burden as it gives them more to sort through and categorize. Other people don't comprehend how difficult it is for Fives to get rid of things that hold meaning for them. This can be a source of tension because their collections can take up so much space.

The root sin for Type Five is avarice or stinginess. They have a "scarcity mentality" and they *fear being depleted of sufficient resources to carry on with life.* Knowing there are limitations to their time, energy, money, and knowledge, they withhold them lest they run out. This includes emotional engagement with others. Staying detached and independent is much safer than entering the unknown realm of emotions where they may be caught off guard and overwhelmed. Intimacy can feel like an intrusion and sacrifice. This doesn't mean they don't experience strong feelings but that they are more likely to evaluate them alone rather than expose them to others. Highly charged situations are paralyzing, even though their steady nature and rational approach are helpful in seeing a way through.

Type Fives avoid looking foolish and uninformed. This compels them to be overly thorough and consider all possible angles on a topic. They prepare 120 percent when they are asked to present something, just in case they run out of material or are faced with a question they can't answer. Their fear of looking foolish also impacts making decisions and taking action. They will do diligent research, but if they sense that a small bit of information is missing, they will sit back and do nothing rather than risk making an unwise choice. This can be about a small purchase, like a home appliance, or a major life decision, such as a career move.

As a part of the Head Center, Type Fives are concerned with safety and security, and they find solace in the arena of their minds. Knowledge gives them power over the fear of not being equipped to able to handle what comes their way. When they feel swallowed up by too many demands on their time and energy, they withdraw into themselves for protection. Since they like to observe life from a distance rather than participate, they can easily hide behind their mask of intellectual pursuits and stay detached from the life going on around them. Others may consider them shy, aloof, or unsociable, but this is how they retreat into their inquiring minds where life is more concrete, predictable, and secure.

Transformative Growth to Freedom

If a person identifies with the personality patterns of Type Five, what qualities of their Authentic Self will emerge as they soften and disown the protective seed coat of their Adapted Self? How will they become more like Jesus as they follow Him?

> My need for isolation was challenged when I became part of a mission community that spent several years traveling together. I learned that a collective "group think" was more valuable and life-giving to me than my own private thoughts. My understanding of love was reorganized as I experienced unconditional acceptance for just being myself without any pretense. Along the way, I was exposed to various expressions of faith, and this opened up a whole new world of discovery and openness to different ways of experiencing God.

Type Fives will experience more generosity, community, and trust when they release their insatiable quest for the knowledge they believe will protect and save them from being swallowed up by a demanding world. They will no longer fear being depleted, but will experience a new freedom to give away what they have. They will offer their gifts of time, energy, and talent with faith in a God who is generous and will meet their needs. In this way, they will become an available resource so people can access their wisdom and expertise.

Fives will become less driven to be self-sufficient and will seek out and enjoy the companionship of others with whom they can share their lives and learn together. Their need for time alone will change from a survival tactic to a desire to contemplate and connect with their own heart and God's presence. When they shift their focus from trying to make sense of things, they allow for mystery and the unknown. Spiritual truths will be experienced as living realities rather than examined as abstract concepts. Their divine gift of inner knowing will equip them to listen for the nudging of God's Spirit and bring their gifts of perception and insight forward to help others know and experience His deeper truths and wisdom.

TYPE FIVE

Divine Gift:	God's wisdom and truth
Core Need:	To perceive and know
Focus of Attention:	What makes sense
Root Sin:	Avarice or stinginess
Avoidance:	Looking foolish or uninformed
Primary Fear:	Being depleted
Transformational Growth:	Generosity and community

Authentic Self	Adapted Self
Redeemed Qualities	**Unredeemed Characteristics**
Curious	Distant
Insightful	Cynical
Interesting	Private
Rational	Unassertive
Witty	Intense
Objective	Miserly
Observant	Isolated
Sensitive	Heady
Persevering	Abstract
Thorough	Self-reliant
Knowledgeable	Overwhelmed

Type Six: A Reflection of God's Faithfulness and Courage

"Be strong and courageous. Do not be afraid or terrified . . . for the LORD your God goes with you; he will never leave you nor forsake you."
—*Deuteronomy 31:6*

"Anxiety's like a rocking chair. It gives you something to do, but it doesn't get you very far."
—*Jodi Picoult*

Those who identify with the Type Six pattern reflect God's faithful and steady presence. They desire to experience the dependable guidance and support that undergirds all of life. Regardless of circumstances, they can access the courage and perseverance to transcend doubt and uncertainty. God's imprint of loyalty is expressed in their supportive commitment to relationships and His reliability is seen in their determination to responsibly carry out whatever they are called upon to do. A Type Six person said:

> I feel settled and at peace when I anchor my life in God, knowing that He is there for me and makes my paths straight. It's exciting to consider myself in partnership with Him—that we are in this life together and I can face whatever comes my way. When I remember all the ways He has been my strong tower, I can take shelter in Him. I feel like a baby bird being cared for by its mother. It's very warm and secure under His wings.

The Authentic Self

At their best, those who identify with Type Six are trustworthy, cooperative, and supportive. They faithfully carry out their responsibilities with integrity and high ethical standards. They make good team players who diligently work to ensure that every practical detail is covered and all loopholes are considered. This can seem like a "wet blanket" to visionaries on a team, but the Sixes' attentiveness to what must get done and what could go wrong is a gift worth embracing. When faced with challenging situations, they keep a level head and have an innate sense of the next steps to be taken. They are skilled trouble-shooters and enjoy assisting others in preparing and executing strategies to resolve perplexing issues. Their warmth and loyal support provide a constant presence of care and stability to their family, friends, coworkers, and the institutions they serve. They will rarely let someone down or fail to fulfill the duties expected of them. Sixes are strong and courageous when they rely on the undergirding guidance and protection of God. When they pay attention to their own inner voice, they can trust themselves to make good decisions and act in accordance with their valued principles. Their solid faith and unwavering fidelity provide a clear picture of God's faithfulness and reliability.

The Adapted Self

Early in their life, those with a Type Six propensity likely experienced an absence of guidance and certainty that created a sense of unsettledness and confusion. Perhaps people whom they counted on to provide a stable environment disappeared or failed to give them support and direction on how to get through life. Or they became aware that the world is a scary place where bad things happen. They wondered who or what could be trusted to take care of them. By paying careful attention to what pleased or displeased authority figures, they determined to obey and carry out expected responsibilities in order to earn a favorable standing with those over them. These childhood experiences and the Six's attunement to faithfulness and certainty resulted in the distorted assumption that *"I must do my duty and follow the rules in order to be secure and avoid harm and punishment.*" Constructing their lives around this lie is a source of suffering for Sixes.

> As a child, I often was left to figure out what to do. I didn't learn the practical things that would have helped me get by in life. I also took on the responsibility of keeping my family from disintegrating. When I was quite young, I overheard my parents say they would divorce when I graduated from high school. I thought then that it would be best if I didn't graduate so they would stay together. I realize now that I've always had a deep down yearning for someone to tell me how to live and show me the way.

The apparent absence of a reliable foundation set in motion a life of protecting themselves from danger and unpredictability by thinking through threats to their survival and well-being. Of the three types in the Head Center, Type Sixes are the most overtly concerned about their safety and security. They sense potential problems at every turn and work hard to be prepared and equipped. At the same time, they have little confidence in their ability to handle difficulties, so they place their trust in those who can and should do it for them. Their gift of loyalty is altered into a dependence on other people or institutions to tell them what to believe, how to behave, and who they should be. At the same time, they question whether people will stay with them for the long haul. They are plagued with self-doubt and fear they will be abandoned if they don't comply with expectations and standards. They even fear that God will punish them if they fail to obey His precepts. Because systems and rules provide them with a false sense of assurance and security, going against them is almost unthinkable.

However, there are two manifestations of the Type Six personality pattern: phobic and counterphobic. These seem quite different in how they respond to authority and how they manage their ever-present anxiety, but they share the same underlying fear. The phobic Six will blindly trust and follow anyone in a position of power or prominence, believing that these authority figures will provide protection and guidance if they respect and obey them. They also want to avoid punishing consequences for non-compliance. The counterphobic Six will challenge and resist structures and authorities to test their strength and see if they can be trusted. They also fear being overrun and hurt by them. The phobic Six manages his or her anxiety by planning and organizing ways to escape harm. The counterphobic Sixes will put themselves in danger and attack their fears rather than be tortured by their troublesome thoughts. The phobic Six is compliant and passive, while the counterphobic is rebellious and aggressive. Although these approaches are different, a Type Six person might employ both strategies at various times.

The focus of attention for Type Six is on what could go wrong. They envision worst-case scenarios and channel their energy toward preventing what they fear could possibly happen. They obsess over a small incident and imagine any number of dreadful outcomes, such as contracting a deadly disease if they accidently touch a drop of blood from an unknown source. They can also conjure up a story in their minds about what someone meant by an offhand comment and how it will affect them. The ability to foresee problems can be a gift to themselves and others, but the incessant anticipation of potential catastrophe can be consuming and paralyzing. This focus is not limited to physical dangers, but includes relationships, finances, projects, God's acceptance, and the like. The exaggerated focus on what might go awry can make them overly cautious, apprehensive, and afraid to step out of their familiar and stable comfort zone.

Thus *the root sin for Type Six is their free-floating anxiety.* They worry about anything and everything. They even make up things to worry about for fear they might miss something. To stop fretting and preparing means they may unexpectedly face something they can't handle. This taps into their *fear of being helpless and defenseless.* They believe something awful is sure to happen if they cease being vigilant and careful. And they're not sure they can cope if it does. When something unfortunate does happen, they often blame themselves for being irresponsible and unprepared. Or they cast blame on those who should have taken care of them. This reinforces their duty to scan and plan for harm and surround themselves with resources that will keep them safe and secure.

> Anxiety feels like a freight train. It's as if I am standing on a platform looking down the track. I can feel the train's vibration and feel it coming, and then find myself completely taken up by it and can't get off. Ten miles down I realize I'm captured by fear. It takes me time to calm down and gain my bearings again.

Since they don't trust their own inner authority, Type Sixes have difficulty making decisions. Even though they are one of the types in the Head Center, their anxiety overrides their rationality and clear thinking. They will seek out the advice of several people and consult numerous resources before making a choice. Similar to listening to the loud inner critic of Type One, a Type Six listens to a strong inner committee of many competing voices. It's a cause for sleepless nights and mental exhaustion. Whom should they trust and how can they know for sure? They would almost rather have someone else choose for them, so they aren't responsible for the consequences. If they do make a decision, they often wonder if it was the right one or if someone more competent would have made a different choice. It's an endless cycle of self-questioning.

Transformative Growth to Freedom

If a person identifies with the personality patterns of Type Six, what qualities of their Authentic Self will emerge as they soften and disown the protective seed coat of their Adapted Self? How will they become more like Jesus as they follow Him? Here's what one Type Six person said:

> I am learning to trust and honor my inner voice. If I have an inkling about something, I will just go with it, realizing that I can

adjust later if I need to. There is such a kindness toward myself in this. When I am more centered and grounded in God and myself, I feel more a part of the divine flow deep within me. I can feel it bubbling up inside, like I'm tapping into the true source of life and my true self.

Type Sixes will experience more confidence, courage, and inner repose as they shift from fretting about uncertainty to trusting the solid support that is always available for them. This support doesn't come from external sources, but from the inner fortitude and wisdom of God and themselves. They will learn to rely less on others to defend and direct them. It can be a bit unsettling to step out and take charge of their own lives, but they will find a new freedom that comes from making decisions and taking action, even if they aren't completely sure. An inner peace will replace their anxious thoughts when they stand in faith on the ground of God's presence, even when circumstances are difficult and uncertain. Acknowledging their fears and finding humor in their runaway imagination of pending doom is a calming antidote to their worried minds.

Sixes will be more energized to offer their talents of common sense, responsibility, and getting things done when they aren't attached to making sure nothing goes wrong. Their gifts of loyalty and support will grow even stronger as they lessen their dependence on others for guidance and security. They will enjoy life more, be willing to take risks, and rest in the faithfulness and strength of God. At the same time, they will access their own inner resources to push through fears and live courageously.

TYPE SIX

Divine Gift:	God's faithfulness and courage
Core Need:	To be safe and certain
Focus of Attention:	What could go wrong
Root Sin:	Anxiety
Avoidance:	Deviance and punishment
Primary Fear:	Being helpless and defenseless
Transformational Growth:	Courage and confidence

Authentic Self	Adapted Self
Redeemed Qualities	Unredeemed Characteristics
Trustworthy	Cautious
Loyal	Timid
Honorable	Controlling
Responsible	Hyper-vigilant
Supportive	Suspicious
Practical	Dependent
Determined	Rigid
Prepared	Indecisive
Cooperative	Ambivalent
Dedicated	Doubtful
Interdependent	Security conscious

Type Seven: A Reflection of God's Joy and Abundance

"You make known to me the path of life;
you will fill me with joy in your presence,
with eternal pleasures at your right hand."
                                        —*Psalm 16:11*

"The two enemies of human happiness are
pain and boredom."
                        —*Arthur Schopenhauer, philosopher*

Those who identify with the pattern of Type Seven reflect the presence of God's joy and redemption in all of life. They envision a bright future where suffering is alleviated and all people are free to enjoy the limitless pleasures God provides. They view the world through a lens of abundance and their enthusiasm is contagious. Type Sevens long to experience God's deep joy and expansiveness and join with others in the adventure of living life to the full. Thoughts of a Type Seven:

> I have a childlike surprise that makes every moment wonderful. It's thrilling to think of possibilities and I don't mind navigating the red tape to make things happen. When a new idea comes to me, I sit up straight, my body twitches, and I am filled with endorphins. There's nothing quite like the joy of planning and pulling off something that is tons of fun and makes people happy.

The Authentic Self

At their best, Type Sevens are playful, curious, and optimistic. Life, from their perspective, is designed to be full of delight and adventure. They are catalysts for joy wherever they go and can turn an ordinary day into an exciting event. Never ones to settle for a humdrum life, they dream about new experiences and practically live them out through their vivid imaginations. They may not follow through on an idea, but they can shift to the next possibility without looking back. Eager to expand their curiosity for life, they devour new ideas, information, insights, and interesting facts. They enjoy getting to know a variety of people and engaging in stimulating conversations. Good food, fine drink, and vibrant surroundings make them feel happy. Their charm and cheerfulness lighten the load of life's difficulties. When circumstances are challenging, they rarely get bogged down because they know hardships will soon pass and everything will be okay. They encourage others to keep a balanced perspective on the positive outcomes of seemingly negative situations, offering alternatives to the "gloom and doom" mindset. As messengers of God's joy and abundance, they are alive to every moment and embrace with enthusiasm all the good things life has to offer.

The Adapted Self

For those who long to experience a vast range of fun and possibilities, being limited by the restrictions and realities of life was frustrating to young Type Sevens. They couldn't do or have everything they wanted; this was experienced as a loss of freedom and a barrier to their happiness. So they devised ways to escape the monotony of everyday life, uninteresting people, and tedious responsibilities. External activities and vivid fantasies filled up their days and nights so they wouldn't have to feel the pain of being confined. And they found it was fun and fulfilling to play and imagine and dream, especially with the company of others. These childhood experiences and the inherent zest for life of the Type Seven developed into the false notion that *"I will be satisfied and happy if I stay busy, enjoy all the pleasures in life, and keep a positive outlook."* Constructing their lives around this lie is a source of suffering for Sevens.

My home life was very narrow and boring. I spent most of my days in the woods near our home with my friends. We built forts, invented fun things to do, and made up adventures. One day, my mother gave me a sticker book with pictures of monuments around the world. I suddenly realized there was another world out there for me to discover. I began to learn everything I could. I dreamed of traveling the world, which I've done. That sticker book touched a nerve in me that I've never forgotten.

The longing for freedom and the awareness of limitations set in motion a life of re-creating pleasure and possibilities for Type Sevens. They ponder an array of options and often have difficulty picking just one. All of the options are appealing and choosing one means eliminating others. This can result in a resistance to commitments that tie them down. Sevens can seem flighty and distracted, but it's because they bounce from one thing to another quite rapidly, mostly in their busy minds. So much captures their attention and they want to experience it all. Variety and constant stimulation make them feel alive, but this can tire others around them out. Sevens can be impatient and impulsive, ready to grasp whatever will make their life happier and more exciting.

Thus for Type Sevens, *the focus of attention is on "what's next?"* They expend their energy making plans for an exciting future, even for the next hour. As one of the types in the Head Center, this scheming happens in their active and imaginative minds. To be without options is frightening. Many of their ideas may not come to pass, but even dreaming about them is half the fun. This can present a challenge in their close relationships if someone dampens their enthusiasm about something they want to have or do. When someone puts a kibosh on their ideas, they feel frustrated and sad at having to compromise. It's one thing to accept that something's impossible, but it's another if they see thwarted opportunities as a lack of vision and an unwillingness to take risks. Letting go of their dreams feels like a death and they often create a substitute for what they missed.

The tendency to orchestrate what's ahead is related to their *fear of being trapped and deprived.* They always want an escape route available in case they are caught in a mundane conversation or an unpleasant situation. If there isn't a way out physically, they wander off in their minds to a more exciting thought. When faced with a potentially boring day, they throw in something fun to make it more endurable. They put off tedious tasks until they are pressed, and then it feels like such an imposition to get them done. This makes it difficult for Type Sevens to be content with their present circumstances as their imagined future is much more captivating. One Type Seven put it this way:

> It's easy for me to be caught up in ideas about a new endeavor and impulsively get going on it without thinking it through very much. Then I have to follow up and do the hard work to keep it going. That's not much fun and feels like drudgery. I always need to create new incentives so I will stay motivated to stick with anything.

The root sin for Type Seven is gluttony or insatiability. This is not just about food, but about their appetite for more and more pleasure. They never feel like they have enough to be fully satisfied. The result is an excessive pursuit of what they think will fill up their inner void and make them happy. This can be food and drink, activities, relationships, information, travel, music, laughter, movies, clothes, possessions, and on the list goes. For a Seven, there is no end to this hunger and craving for more. But they rarely feel full.

Since Sevens long to experience the best in life, *they avoid pain and suffering.* They can accept that life is hard sometimes, but they see no reason to wallow in it. They try to figure out redemptive solutions so people don't have to experience suffering. And they think everyone can choose to be happy regardless of their circumstances. They will stay by the side of someone who is hurting, but their empathy is cool and distant internally. This doesn't mean they're cold-hearted, but they don't access their emotions or even recognize they have them. Their avoidance of pain is really an avoidance of their own shadow side. They deny parts of themselves they don't want to see by keeping their lives busy, engaged, and moving on to the next thing. In this way, their hurts, anger, disappointments, and discouragements will not surface and disrupt their happiness. Why dig up painful things if it dampens their positive outlook and hopeful optimism? Focusing on the dark side of life makes no sense to a Seven since there is so much to embrace and enjoy.

Like the other types in the Head Center, Sevens are anxious and concerned with their safety and security. This is not so much about coping with external dangers or limited resources but about the fear of being overtaken and paralyzed by their own negative feelings, painful memories, and unmet longings. Occupying their minds with plans and distractions keeps them safe from themselves and their own internal landscape. Also they hope their optimistic and fun-loving approach to life will make others like them and want to be with them. Security in relationships means shared experiences and enlightening interactions. It also means no one is upset or unhappy with them. This can come across as trying too hard and can have the opposite effect of overwhelming people with their enthusiasm and abundance of ideas.

Transformative Growth to Freedom

If a person identifies with the personality patterns of Type Seven, what qualities of their Authentic Self will emerge as they soften and disown the protective seed coat of their Adapted Self? How will they become more like Jesus as they follow Him?

> I am learning to stay with sadness and suffering. I used to ignore these hard feelings, but I realize now that I missed out on some deeper parts of life. I don't really like to notice suffering because it feels bad. But I now sense a larger capacity to hold the pain of

others in a genuine and healing way. I'm also not afraid to slow down and allow God to be with me in my own struggles.

Type Sevens will experience more sustained joy, gratitude, and awe in the present moment when they release their driving need to fill their lives with pleasure and plans. They will learn to embrace all of life, the unpleasant along with the enjoyable. To their surprise, they will discover a deeper joy when they accept and allow pain and limitations, as well as admit their own negative qualities. They will come to know the abiding and redemptive presence of God in the midst of what might seem intolerable. And His grace will be more evident. Their view of life will be more subdued and sober, but they will sense a new freedom to experience the spectrum of emotions from delight to sorrow. This may be uncomfortable, but they will find a fullness of life they could not otherwise know if they kept their emotional life at bay. And they will find a new capacity to genuinely be with others in their pain and struggles.

As Sevens pause and quiet their busy and scheming minds, they will come to notice and appreciate the wonder of what they already have in the here and now. Today will be enough and they will feel satisfied. As reflections of God's joy and abundance, they will always enrich their lives and the lives of others with exciting adventures, engaging conversations, and endless fun, but without the insatiable search for what might fill the void only God can fill.

TYPE SEVEN

Divine Gift:	God's joy and abundance
Core Need:	To be happy and free
Focus of Attention:	What's next
Root Sin:	Gluttony or insatiability
Avoidance:	Pain and suffering
Primary Fear:	Being trapped and deprived
Transformational Growth:	Sober joy and groundedness

Authentic Self	Adapted Self
Redeemed Qualities	Unredeemed Characteristics
Optimistic	Impulsive
Enthusiastic	Superficial
Spontaneous	Distracted
Charming	Escapist
Imaginative	Restless
Versatile	Unreliable
Entertaining	Indecisive
Visionary	Reckless
Curious	Inconsistent
Engaging	Excessive
Playful	Flighty

Type Eight: A Reflection of God's Power and Protection

"Yours, Lord, is the greatness and the power and the glory and the majesty and the splendor, for everything in heaven and in earth is yours. . . . In your hands are strength and power to exalt and give strength to all."
—*1 Chronicles 29:11-12*

"If you lose a big fight, it will worry you all of your life. It will plague you—until you get your revenge."
—*Muhammad Ali*

Those who identify with Type Eight reflect God's power and strength and have a deep desire to experience the aliveness of the original human state—full of passion, purpose, and protection for all. The imprinted image of God on their very being is to empower the powerless and bring about justice in an unjust world. They long to be connected to the vitality of God's greatness and the weight of His glory. Their deepest longing is to experience and express the divine gift of God's power and might. A Type Eight said:

I feel most connected to God when I'm operating like a hose connected to a spigot—when His forcefulness flows through me to others. I sense His strength and know I'm being used for His purposes. I want to be aligned with God's passion for people and exercise my leadership gifts to stand with the helpless and provide opportunities for them to grow and reach their full potential. There is nothing quite as exhilarating as witnessing someone rise above their difficult circumstances and accomplish something they never dreamed they could.

The Authentic Self

At their best, Eights are crusaders for justice, dynamic leaders, and protectors of the vulnerable. They have a passion for life and love that runs through their veins and they are fun and inspiring to be around. They direct their energies toward mobilizing people to work for causes of justice and create opportunities for those without resources to thrive in society. They are bold, straightforward, fearless, and confident. At the same time, they welcome the challenge to think and act outside of their normal routine and held beliefs, and they enjoy lively discussions about topics of interest to them. When an Eight's heart of mercy is combined with their capable leadership, they inspire great movements of positive change for the world. They have an intuitive sense of what needs to be done quickly and effectively to make things happen.

Type Eights enjoy many treasured relationships and invest their time and energy to build trusting commitments with their intimate partners, close friends, and co-laborers. They will stick with someone for life and be a constant champion of their success and fulfillment. Although they appear strong and confident on the outside, they have a soft and tender heart on the inside. Closeness and vulnerability don't come easily for an Eight, but once they let someone in, they can express true tenderness and care.

The Adapted Self

In an unjust and cruel world, the young Eights inevitably suffered betrayal, rejection, or being undermined by someone's dominance. They fought to stand up for themselves and tried to be tough-skinned, yet their experiences of being challenged or wounded affected them deeply. Behind the bravado of an Eight is the tender heart of a little boy or girl who feels vulnerable. They adapted to their hidden hurt by erecting a guard of self-protection to guarantee they wouldn't be hurt again. Because of their innate attunement to strength, they were also sensitive to the disparities of power and privilege, such as bullying on the playground. From their childhood experiences and their innate understanding of power they came to believe that *"I must be strong and invincible to survive in a hostile world where the powerful take advantage of the weak."* Constructing their lives around this lie is a source of suffering for Eights.

> I always found myself sticking up for the underdog. One of my friends was picked on by a group of guys, so I beat one of them up. Later, another came up and smashed my face and broke my nose. I was kicked out of school twice for starting a fight, but it always seemed like the right thing to do—to stand up for the ones who couldn't do it for themselves. I just couldn't stay back and do nothing.

The drive of Eights to be strong and resilient set in motion a life of re-creating power and protection for themselves and others. They over-identify with their divine gift of power and can misuse it to dominate others and establish a position of strength so as not to appear weak. They adopted a "me against the world" stance in life and embraced the lie that "only the strong survive."

Thus *the focus of attention for Type Eight is on taking charge.* This lines up with the need for power and control of the Gut Center Types. Their forceful energy is directed toward addressing and attacking anything that might threaten their influence and power. Quite often, their first response to a suggestion or opposing idea is "no." Eights are invigorated by an honest conflict that gets everything out on the table, and they fight for their position with unrelenting intensity. They may change their mind, but the argument for a differing opinion has to be sound and convincing. In fact, a heated head-to-head confrontation can feel very intimate to them, even though the other person might walk away wounded.

Eights move quickly and decisively and want to get things done pronto. They are impatient and frustrated with inaction. As part of a team, they become restless if they're not in charge, progress is slow, or their ideas aren't valued. This forces them to tone down their energy and keep silent, but they will feel like a ticking time bomb inside. They often take command anyway and this can either be welcomed or resented.

If an Eight is not in a position of authority, he or she will figure out who is in charge and muscle their way to befriend the powers that be. This gives them a sense of security and protection so they won't be overcome and lose their influence. Their contact with those in control also gives them an opening to garner support for the benefit of those who are oppressed and the projects to which they are committed. They will knock on the doors of the rich and powerful and they usually get what they ask for.

Eights tend to be competitive, self-confident, and independent. Life, for them, is a battleground; their armor is on and they stand ready to fight and stand their ground. Winning is paramount and losing is devastating. It takes them a long time to recover from defeat and they either bury it or figure out a way to come out on top next time. If they feel undermined or betrayed by someone, they cut them off and attempt to get back at them somehow. A battle isn't over until the Eight is satisfied with a win of some kind.

A battle also exists inside where they struggle with their own unresolved emotions and fears. They avoid being vulnerable and appearing weak. They vacillate between their need to keep people at a distance and their longing to be close. Their role in society to protect the unprotected and defend the defenseless is also a reflection of their *own fear of being exposed, disrespected, and taken advantage of.* They wrestle to express their tender heart, but the possibility of being hurt can hold them back. Coming to grips with their emotional life is a lifelong struggle.

> People don't know how much I hurt and that my underbelly is very soft. I don't realize how strong and capable I appear to people. I think I intimidate them and come across as abrasive. But I feel

lonely and deeply long to be embraced by others. I guess I don't
let them see the cry of my heart very often. Exposing my soft side
is frightening. And when I've been hurt or my intentions have
been questioned, I will retreat and put my guard up so I won't
be hurt again.

The root sin or vice for Type Eight is lust and shamelessness. Their
appetite to live large and experience all the gusto they can often
leads to uncontrolled excessiveness in their lives. They like to break
the rules and push against restrictive boundaries. A "no trespassing"
sign doesn't apply to them and will make them want to trespass just
to prove they can. Their need for control is so dominant that they
will prevail over others for their own ends. They want to call the
shots and exert pressure on those who resist them. This pattern of
shamelessness will get them into trouble in relationships and work,
and it may end up backfiring on them in the end.

As with the other Gut types, Eights wrestle with their underlying
anger. For them, it's forceful and felt, not only by themselves but
by others. They are surprised that people aren't always comfortable
with its intensity. Their fury is ignited when they are disrespected,
left in the dark about things that affect them, suffer humiliation, or
feel unprotected. They also have deeply felt anger about injustice and
the mistreatment of people and have little patience for the apathy of
people who don't seem to care. If the rage of an Eight isn't under
control, he or she can be mean and combative. When their anger
is tempered, it can become a positive source of power and an agent
of change in the world.

Transformative Growth to Freedom

If a person identifies with the personality patterns of Type Eight,
what qualities of their Authentic Self will emerge as they disown
and soften the protective seed coat of their Adapted Self? How will

they become more like Jesus as they follow Him? Here are some
thoughts of a Type Eight:

> I'm learning to forgive and ask others to forgive me. The Lord
> will nudge me to reach out to someone I've hurt in the past and
> admit I was wrong. He also leads me to connect with people I've
> dismissed because I felt betrayed by them. It's not always easy or
> comfortable for me. But when I do, I recognize the hurt in them
> and that I was at fault too. My heart will soften and it feels good
> to restore a broken relationship.

Type Eights will experience more childlikeness, tenderness, and a new,
quiet strength as they release their need to be in control and protect
themselves against any opposition. As they experience freedom to
allow the truth of their own helplessness to surface, they will notice
a growing gentleness and compassion for the wounded child within.
This is where they will know the healing embrace of God and a return
to innocence and grace. By sharing their true heart with others, they
will realize it isn't as scary as they thought it would be. In fact, softness
will replace the hard shell of protection and they will experience more
honesty, trust, and intimacy in their relationships. To their surprise,
they find true strength in being vulnerable and a greater capacity to
empathize with others who struggle. Rather than dismissing criticism
and rejecting their critics, they will welcome the opportunity to listen,
change their ways, and reconcile with those they may have hurt.

As reflections of God's true power and strength, Eights who
have relaxed their own clamor for power and influence can effect
great change for the oppressed and mistreated. When they shift their
focus from taking charge and being contentious to collaboration
and agreement, they will be more effective in their efforts to inspire
others to join in the fight against injustice. As they let go of their
need for control, they can channel their dynamic energy into
empowering others, demonstrating mercy, and living self-controlled
and passionate lives.

TYPE EIGHT

Divine Gift:	God's power and protection
Core Need:	To be in control
Focus of Attention:	Taking charge
Root Sin:	Lust or shamelessness
Avoidance:	Vulnerability and weakness
Primary Fear:	Being exposed and disrespected
Transformational Growth:	Tenderness and grace

Authentic Self	Adapted Self
Redeemed Qualities	**Unredeemed Characteristics**
Inspiring	Forceful
Just	Loud
Protective	Vengeful
Compassionate	Possessive
Energetic	Intimidating
Resilient	Insensitive
Direct	Domineering
Confident	Rebellious
Assertive	Excessive
Influential	Combative
Empowering	Explosive

Type Nine: A Reflection of God's Peace and Oneness

"Peace I leave with you; my peace I give you.
I do not give to you as the world gives.
Do not let your hearts be troubled and do not be afraid."
—*John 14:27*

"I was going to do something today,
but I haven't finished doing nothing from yesterday."
—*Unknown*

Those who identify with Type Nine reflect God's blending of all things into a peaceful harmony. They have a deep desire to experience the original connectivity of the human state where nothing is separated and every part is essential to the whole. The imprinted image of God on their very being is for all people and things to be together in one accord. They long for a time when they experience an inner state of well-being that is undisturbed and at rest. This is their deepest longing—to experience and express the divine gift of God's true peace.

> I feel most alive when I feel joined together with something. This may be with another person in a heart-to-heart conversation, in nature where I feel united with creation, or in situations where I empathize with what someone is going through. I enjoy my oneness with God in solitude and in the activities that flow out of solitude, like gardening. For me, it's all about the sense of being connected.

The Authentic Self

At their best, Nines are warm, adaptable, and unpretentious. They are natural peacemakers who work to resolve conflicts by accepting and valuing different points of view and discovering a common thread of consensus. For this reason, they are gifted listeners and mediators. Their easygoing nature brings balance to tumultuous situations. They are composed, patient, and able to let things unfold on their own. With Nines, you get what you see as they rarely have a hidden agenda. They enjoy the comfort of stress-free living and don't take life too seriously. They don't tend to draw attention to themselves, although they will take the stage when they are given an opening. When Nines have clarity and become focused on an endeavor, they step into action, get things done without much fuss, and are hard to stop. They are not easily offended and step away from conflict to maintain inner repose. Nines experience contentment when they are in harmony with others and when their energy is channeled to a particular calling that makes a significant contribution. A Type Nine reflected:

> I like being who I am. I like the ease of it and I'm not stressed out all the time like other people. I like being the person who can bypass difficulties and can be helpful in times of struggle or tension without taking on the burdens of others too much. Life is just easier that way.

The Adapted Self

The relaxed temperament of Nines made it easy for them to blend in and make themselves invisible as they were developing as children. When inevitable conflicts arose in their personal lives, they could disappear and wait until the issue resolved itself or blew over. If they expressed strong feelings, they often felt reprimanded or overlooked for speaking up, especially if this created tension. This sense of strife was experienced as a painful separation from others because of their hardwired desire for unity. They learned to downplay themselves and their emotions to avoid conflict and trouble. They were also praised as easygoing children who didn't demand much attention. As a result, they came to believe that *"I must be calm and go along with others to stay connected and comfortable."* Constructing their lives around this lie is a source of suffering for Nines.

The Nine's desire for peace and harmony set in motion a life of re-creating rest and comfort by blocking out what disturbs their inner repose. Nines over-identify with their gift of peace and oneness by being unflappable and yielding to others. They don't allow themselves to get too worked up about much of anything and seem oblivious to the harsh realities of life. It is said that Nines "make molehills out of mountains." This can come across as apathetic and complacent. They are cynical toward others who are stressed and over-reactive to life's circumstances. They don't like being pushed or bothered with obligations they don't want to fulfill. They take the path of least resistance to stay in their comfort zone. Nines assume that everything will work out anyway, so why bother to put forth unnecessary energy to make something happen. This tamped-down approach to life may be comfortable, but they also miss out on much of what goes on around them.

This also leads to a numbing out of their emotions. Because they work hard to avoid strife by controlling their anger and frustrations, they also close off other feelings like joy and love and sadness. They hold back tears and distract themselves from feeling too deeply for fear of being overwhelmed and out of control. Most Nines want to experience more emotions, but have limited access to them. This is an outcome of their strategy to avoid conflict. Discord goes against their self-image of being settled and unruffled.

The focus of attention for Type Nines is on what others want or expect from them. They direct their energy toward adjusting their lives to the spoken or unspoken agendas of others. They don't want to rock the boat or create discord, so they set aside their own plans to accommodate others. As a result, they're often not in touch with their own desires and priorities. They have a hard time speaking up for themselves and are often not very clear on what they really want anyway. It's easier just to go along with others rather than do the hard work of knowing and expressing their own preferences. By this, they strive to keep the peace and avoid feeling separated from the people in their lives.

Thus the root sin for Type Nine is sloth or indolence. These words can imply laziness, but most Nines seem busy. It really means an inattentiveness to their own priorities; they often don't even know what they are. They can spend hours wandering from one activity to another without a clear sense of purpose or intention. They are easily called away from what they set out to do by another demand or distraction. Setting goals and priorities can feel like a source of conflict because they have to make choices that may disappoint others. It's hard work for them to know what they really want in life or what their calling might be. The lack of connection to their own inner life reduces internal and external conflict but also creates a disjointed array of activities with no central focus. The result is personal negligence, lack of direction, and trouble taking the first step to getting something accomplished. Thoughts of a Type Nine:

> This is my biggest struggle. I can be on my own road and the next thing I know I'm on someone else's road without even being aware of how I got swept away. Sometimes I feel like I'm bouncing around—doing what I'm expected to do—but not necessarily living how I want to live. I'm learning to check in with myself more. Am I on my agenda or on their agenda—and is that okay with me for a time? I need to ask if I am giving up too much of myself for the priorities of someone else.

As a type in the Gut Center, Nines attempt to meet their need for power and control by an internal stubbornness few people see. They may be going along with others on the outside but not necessarily on the inside. Because they *fear being invisible and insignificant,* they tenaciously cling to part of themselves lest they dissolve completely into the lives of others. This is true in their relationship with God. They fear that surrendering to Him means they stop existing somehow or they will have to give away all of themselves to be of use to Him. So they hold out. This creates an uncomfortable disharmony in which they feel they are pretending to be one way when in fact their inner experience is another way. This is how they maintain a sense of control while they continue to be dominated by the wants and expectations of others.

The nature of anger for Nines is passive-aggressive. They go along and comply with others and at the same time feel dismissed and devalued. They are particularly hurt when they don't feel heard or are overlooked, reinforcing their fear of being unimportant. They will ruminate inside and contain their feelings to avoid creating a problem. This will build up and eventually be expressed in rambling complaints or an angry explosion of words. Others are surprised by the intensity of their pent-up feelings and don't often know how to respond to this uncharacteristic behavior of the peaceful Nine. If someone pulls away from them, they sense the separation they fear. Once a Nine has vented, he or she will retreat and feel a sense of embarrassment at having created a disturbance. Nines pull back into their own inner world, resigning to their held belief that they must acquiesce in order to stay connected.

Transformative Growth to Freedom

If a person identifies with the personality patterns of Type Nine, what qualities of their Authentic Self will emerge as they disown and soften the protective seed coat of their Adapted Self? How will they become more like Jesus as they follow Him? Here are some thoughts of a Type Nine:

> I'm learning to pay attention to myself and value what's important to me. I have to pause and consider what I want and if it matters enough to me to voice it. I don't mind going along with other people and what they want, as long as I'm in touch with why I'm doing it. Is it because I'm afraid of conflict or because I honestly don't care? Most of the time, I'm pretty flexible, and I like being that way. It's when I stand up for myself and my desires that I

need to trust it will turn out okay and that people won't turn away from me.

Type Nines will experience more autonomy, tranquility, and engagement in purposeful action when they release their fear of being disconnected and disruptive if they choose their own path. They will learn to hear their own voice and give attention to their own development and wholeness. Although it feels disorienting at first, they will experience an inner resolve when they define their own dreams and desires and step out to pursue them. They will even discover that, with cooperation and collaboration, their priorities can be on an equal plane with the priorities of others without creating the separation they dread. This will require them to stand up and press through the resistance they feel from within and without. As they shift their focus from doing what other people want to doing what's important to them and what they believe God has called them to do, they will be surprised to realize that the contribution they make will be significant and needed.

Type Nines who have learned to live from their own centered congruence will become agents of reconciliation, offer a calming presence in a world of turmoil, and be receptive to the gamut of emotions felt by themselves and others. They will embrace conflict as a means of growth and a way toward greater connection with others once they push through toward an agreement. They will remain steady and serene, not as way of escaping discomfort and maintaining inner control, but as a reflection of God's peace and desired accord among people.

TYPE NINE

Divine Gift:	God's peace and oneness
Core Need:	To be comfortable and settled
Focus of Attention:	Agenda of others
Root Sin:	Sloth or indolence
Avoidance:	Conflict
Primary Fear:	Being invisible and insignificant
Transformational Growth:	Engagement and autonomy

Authentic Self	Adapted Self
Redeemed Qualities	**Unredeemed Characteristics**
Easygoing	Indifferent
Content	Spaced-out
Receptive	Apathetic
Diplomatic	Passive-aggressive
Guileless	Indecisive
Patient	Uncommitted
Unpretentious	Detached
Open-minded	Appeasing
Down to earth	Obstinate
Reassuring	Neglectful
Accepting	Resigned

8

ARROWS, WINGS, AND SUBTYPES

As I mentioned previously, there are additional components to the system that may seem to make it more complicated, but in fact, can open it up and make it more clear and applicable. Quite often, taking a look at these elements will help a person determine their dominant type if they are unsure. These also illustrate the interrelationships between the nine points, dispelling the concern that this system narrows a person to only one style of personality. Remember my illustration of paint colors? There are the primary colors, but the shades made possible by combining colors are endless. Consider the Arrows and Wings as the tints of other types that create your specific "color." The Subtypes are a bit different, but they are also an important part of most Enneagram teachings.

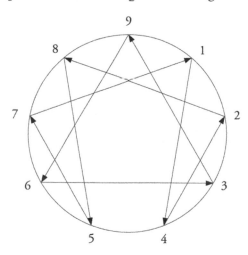

The Arrows

As you can see on the drawing, there are arrows connecting the numbers. Each type has two arrows, one that points toward it and one that points away. These are called by various names: security and stress points, paths of integration and disintegration, true or false consolations. For the sake of simplicity, I will call them security and stress points; the arrow coming toward a number is the security point and the arrow going away is the stress point.

Confusing, yes, but keep reading.

When we feel secure, at ease, and confident, we manifest many of the redeemed and higher qualities of the personality type at the end of the arrow pointing toward our type. An awareness of what we're like when we're secure and relaxed is an indication of our growth to freedom in Christ and the emergence of our Authentic Self. As we surrender to God and are transformed, we will notice the presence and development of the positive qualities of our security point, much to our delight and surprise. This doesn't mean we are to try and imitate the characteristics of our security point or adopt a self-improvement plan to become more like the qualities it represents. Rather, it's as if the divine gifts of this point are drawn toward us as we release the hold on our Adapted Self.

In the other direction is our stress point, the arrow going away from our type. When we are under stress, insecure, and uptight, we will manifest some of the unredeemed qualities of the stress point. I call it our automatic downhill slide. An awareness of our reactions to stress can be a warning sign of a tight grip on our Adapted Self and our resistance to disowning it. Paying attention to this can serve as a reminder to let go. However, stress is inevitable in life and not all stress is negative or paralyzing. This point can also be considered a resource for managing stress and regaining composure by accessing the more positive qualities of the point. So it's not bad or meant to be ignored. In fact, recognizing it is quite helpful. As we surrender to God and are transformed, many of our reactions to stress, which are similar to the less positive characteristics of our stress point, will soften and be less exaggerated or disruptive.

To help clarify this Arrow business, here's how it works for me as a Nine. My security point—the arrow toward Nine—is Type Three. My stress point—the arrow away from Nine—is Type Six. When I'm secure and relaxed, I like who I am, I'm aware of what I want, and I sense a significant purpose, I think and behave like a redeemed Three. I set goals, I'm motivated, I confidently lead, I'm engaged, and I get things done efficiently and effectively. These characteristics just show up when I'm relaxed, trusting, and focused.

On the other hand, when I'm stressed, overwhelmed, feel disregarded and invisible, and allow the agenda of others to dictate my schedule, I'm more like an unredeemed Six. I'm anxious, afraid, unsure of myself, doubt my value, and become paralyzed and unable to act without consulting others for direction. That's just what happens when I'm stressed out. At the same time, I might access the courage and responsibility of Type Six to move me out of my fear. Again, the influence of these two Arrows adds to my unique Nine "color."

The Wings

The Wings are the types located on each side of a number. For example, on one side of Eight is the Seven and on the other side is the Nine, forming the two Wings of Type Eight. For the Five, the Wings are Four and Six.

The influence of the Wings is important to consider as they provide nuance and dimension to the dominant personality type. I think of them like the wings of an airplane, giving balance and a leaning toward one direction or the other. Some experts teach that we only have one Wing that affects us. You will hear people identify themselves, for instance, as a Four with a Three Wing or 4w3. Personally, I think both Wings are important to consider. One of them is usually stronger, but from my own personal experience and my work with others, the other also comes into play.

So how do the Wings influence our personality type? I will use myself as an example. I identify with Type Nine. However, I have a predominant One Wing that flavors how my Nine personality operates and is expressed. I have strong convictions about right and wrong, I desire the ideal, I get things done, and I'm responsible and ethical. I also can be judgmental, resentful, and afraid of criticism. I could be a Type One, yet my easygoing nature and subdued energy wins out if too much effort is required to be perfect, disciplined, and right. On the other side is my Eight Wing. This comes into play when I sense injustice. Just watch me at a sporting event when the referee makes a bad call against my team. I'm the first to protest and seethe with anger at the unfairness. And I'm competitive and hate to lose. Although this is uncharacteristic of my calm Nine style, it will rise to the surface and explode if my "unfair button" is pushed. Yet when I'm not personally invested, I usually cheer for the underdog. I'm influenced by the patterns of both my One and Eight Wings, and the interplay of both on my dominant pattern makes me a unique "color" of Nine.

When we include the Arrows and Wings, our personality pattern is actually a combination of five types rather than just one. We have our primary Type, our two Arrows, and our two Wings. And the connection around the circle even connects us to all the types. The fluidity of these elements gives a dynamic flow, rather than a static state, to the value of the Enneagram.

It's likely that you identify with more than one Enneagram type but aren't sure which one is your most preferred. Take a look at the drawing and notice the types with which you relate. Are they connected by Arrows and/or Wings? Consider how you are when you're secure and when you experience stress. Consider the influence of types adjoining each other. Out of your choices, which one seems to stand out as *most* like you and your life experience?

The Subtypes

One last variant often used is called the Subtypes. These are based on three biological instincts for human survival. We need all of them and we utilize all of them, but they are at differing degrees of importance to us. The three instincts are: 1) Self-Preservation, 2) One-to-One Relationship, and 3) Social Connection. We tend to focus on one of these instincts more than the other two, particularly when it seems threatened. As this applies to the Enneagram, the expression of our dominant type is "colored" by which instinct is of greatest concern to us.

The Self-Preservation instinct is concerned with one's physical comfort and safety, like food, shelter, water, protection, clothing, home, and health. These are the people who always pack a snack, have a bottle of water on hand, and bring an extra coat. They also are concerned with the comfort of their environment, like the temperature, furniture, lighting, and safety from harm. In addition, they put effort into having enough money, securing their future, making plans, and aligning themselves with people who provide for them in emergencies or times of scarcity.

The One-to-One instinct is mainly driven by the need for intimate and intense connections and experiences. As a human survival strategy for a tribe, two people need to come together to create a new person to ensure the group will carry on. In a similar way, those with a focus on the One-to-One instinct will long to create something new with someone else as a sign of connection and intimacy. This is not just about procreation but anything that is experienced together and flows out of the attraction and magnetism of close relationships.

The Social Instinct is concerned with the health and well-being of the entire tribe because if the tribe is doing well, then they are too. They view their survival as part of a broader community rather than individual relationships. Therefore, they work to cultivate a variety of social groups in which they are accepted, supported, and valued. They band together with people who are committed to similar intentions and interests to ensure camaraderie and connection. Those with a strong Social Instinct will work for the overall welfare of the group so it will continue to provide belonging and security for them.

How does this information apply? Simply put, it creates twen-
ty-seven variations, or Subtypes, of the nine main types (three instincts
per each type). Once a person identifies their primary Enneagram
type, they can further examine the Subtypes to understand how their
preferred survival instinct affects their type. It's worth exploring in
more detail, but I don't advise doing it if you are a beginner with the
system. One interesting side note regarding the Subtypes: I've heard
that differences between people on which instinct is most important
to them is a cause for more relational struggles than being a different
type. This might be something to consider as you reflect on particular
disagreements that often arise in your close relationships.

A Summary of the Nine Enneagram Types

9. Divine Gift: PEACE
Need: To be Settled
Focus: Agenda of others
Root Sin: Sloth
Avoid: Conflict
Fear: Being Insignificant
Growth: Engagement
Secure Pt.(3) Focused
Stress Pt.(6): Doubtful

8. Divine Gift: POWER
Need: To be in Control
Focus: Taking charge
Root Sin: Lust
Avoid: Vulnerability
Fear: Being Exposed
Growth: Tenderness
Secure Pt.(2): Altruistic
Stress Pt.(5): Withdrawn

1. Divine Gift: GOODNESS
Need: To be Perfect
Focus: What's wrong?
Root Sin: Resentment
Avoid: Criticism
Fear: Being Unworthy
Growth: Patience
Secure Pt.(7): Spontaneous
Stress Pt.(4): Moody

7. Divine Gift: JOY
Need: To be Free
Focus: What's next?
Root Sin: Gluttony
Avoid: Pain/Suffering
Fear: Being Trapped
Growth: Sober Joy
Secure Pt.(5): Grounded
Stress Pt.(1): Complaining

2. Divine Gift: LOVE
Need: To be Needed
Focus: Other's needs
Root Sin: Pride
Avoid: Own Neediness
Fear: Being Useless
Growth: Humility
Secure Pt.(4): Self-Caring
Stress Pt.(8) Domineering

6. Divine Gift: FAITHFULNESS
Need: To be Certain
Focus: Worst Case/Danger
Root Sin: Anxiety/Worry
Avoid: Deviance
Fear: Being Defenseless
Growth: Courage
Secure Pt.(9): Serene
Stress Pt.(3) Frenetic

3. Divine Gift: HOPE
Need: To Succeed
Focus: Tasks and Goals
Root Sin: Vanity/Deceit
Avoid: Failure
Fear: Being Incapacitated
Growth: Truthfulness
Secure Pt.(6): Trusting
Stress Pt.(9) Paralyzed

5. Divine Gift: WISDOM
Need: To be Perceptive
Focus: What makes sense?
Root Sin: Avarice/Greed
Avoid: Foolishness
Fear: Being Depleted
Growth: Generosity
Secure Pt.(8): Assertive
Stress Pt.(7) Impulsive

4. Divine Gift: DEPTH
Need: To be Special
Focus: What's Missing?
Root Sin: Envy
Avoid: Ordinariness
Fear: Being Unnoticed
Growth: Contentment
Secure Pt.(1): Balanced
Stress Pt(2): Martyr-like

9

HEARING GOD'S PERSONAL INVITATION OF LOVE

"We are called to taste and to touch the embrace of God. Through venturing into the true self, we come to understand that love is truly the only currency that matters and that receiving God's love is our primary responsibility. Only when God's love has been genuinely received can the true self be called out and enabled to give away this love in worshipful living."
—Judith Hougen, *Transformed into Fire*

Pause for a moment to reflect on the embrace of God's love for you in light of all you've discovered about yourself so far. Imagine being rooted and grounded in His transforming presence, surrounded by the fertile soil of His abundant love. The following pages offer possible invitations from God for each particular personality type. As you slowly read and savor them, notice what stirs in your heart and what longings arise as you consider these questions:

- Do you sense the freedom available to you as God draws you toward the center of His love?
- What seed coat obstacles and false beliefs are you invited to disown and release?
- What new life is sprouting as your protective cover falls off?
- Do you glimpse the unique image of God imprinted on you and the possibilities for its expression in the world?
- How might you respond to this invitation of love?

Type One

I invite you to be free from striving to be right and perfect in order to be worthy of My love and approval. You are already worthy and My love for you is a free gift. I'm not judging you; you can stop judging yourself. I invite you to say goodbye to the inner critic that constantly accuses you of not being good enough. I offer you freedom from your judging mind and the burden you carry to correct whatever doesn't live up to your standards. That's My burden and I'm the only one who can make everything right and complete anyway. Acknowledge your simmering anger that the world isn't perfect and you wish it was. I wish it was too, but it isn't.

Accept your imperfections and mistakes and receive My grace and compassion without conditions. Rest and play. I want you to enjoy life with a light and grateful heart. Reclaim your true self that is a glorious reflection of My holiness and righteousness, and move out to offer My goodness and grace to a world that needs it. Use your longing for perfection and your innate gift of seeing what needs to be improved to lovingly make the world a better place in some small way. Freely extend My gentleness, patience, forgiveness, and mercy to everyone I bring your way.

Type Two

I invite you to be free from the belief that you need to help and rescue others to be loved, accepted, and held in high regard. You are simply loved regardless of your contribution. I invite you to release the burden you bear to be the savior for others and to make love happen. That's My job. I offer you freedom from the obligation and panic you feel when the needs of others are made known to you. Trust Me to lead you rather than assuming you must rise to every occasion to be of service. Admit that your pride is based on the belief that you are indispensable and you know best how to care for others. Accept your limitations of time, money, energy, and abilities. Let go of the need to be noticed and appreciated for your selfless service.

Humbly acknowledge your own needs and allow time to take care of yourself without feeling guilty or selfish. And let other people take care of you too. Reclaim your true self that is a glorious reflection of My pure and unconditional love. By releasing your own need to be needed, you will offer My people real love without strings. Recognize that your longing for everyone to experience love and care comes from Me and trust that I will use your innate sensitivity to the needs of others to spread My love to a hurting world.

Type Three

I invite you to be free from the need to succeed in order to establish your worth in the world. You are of great value regardless of your accomplishments. I invite you to release the drive to impress others and depend on their affirmations in order to feel good about yourself. You are not what you do. Your radiance simply rests on the fact that you are My beloved child. I offer you freedom from the tyranny of your goals and tasks; they are useful but they can get in the way of your ability to hear My leading. Trust Me to give you vision and direction.

Admit that you are prone to deceit and boasting in order to portray an image you think others will admire. Accept failure however it comes to you; it's a good teacher and will lead you to more honesty and freedom. Acknowledge that you can't accomplish everything you want and things will get done as they should without your over-involvement to assure success. Listen to your heart and experience your feelings rather than dismissing them as obstacles to your performance. Reclaim your true self that is a bright reflection of My hope and vision for the world. I need you to accomplish My purposes by inspiring others through your innate gifts of leadership and your ability to envision a brighter future for My world and people.

Type Four

I invite you to be free from the drive to be unique and the false belief that you will not be loved and noticed if you don't stand out. You are already extraordinary and special because I created you in love and for love. I invite you to release the fear that you are deficient and something is missing in your life. You have all you need to be content and settled. I offer you freedom from the rise and fall of your emotions as the barometer of your well-being. Embrace your feelings but don't allow them to overwhelm you or shut you off from others. Admit that you are often envious of others and think they have a more fulfilling life than you do. It isn't true. Accept your emotional intensity without expecting others to fully understand you. Let that be okay.

Acknowledge your desire for deep and meaningful connections and recognize they will likely fall short of your idealized yearnings, but don't stop blessing others with your gifts of empathy and sensitivity. Apply your artistry and imagination to express My depth and beauty in ways that touch the hearts of people who long to experience a more real connection with Me and My creativity.

Type Five

I invite you to be free from the fear of scarcity and not having all you need to survive. Trust Me. You will not run out. I'm a generous and loving God who is mindful of all your needs. Accept My sufficiency and receive My provisions with open hands and a willingness to give them away if I ask. Your security rests in Me, not in your own resources. I offer freedom from the fear of looking foolish and uninformed. You can't know everything. People appreciate your brilliant mind and breadth of knowledge, so keep teaching even if you don't feel equipped and valued. Trust that I have given you the mind of Christ and I will direct your thoughts.

Please don't keep Me at a distance because you can't understand everything about Me. My knowledge is too vast and My mysteries are too intricate to be fully comprehended. Yet you and I can still know each other deeply. Allow other people to know your inner world even if it's scary and uncomfortable. You have much to give them and they have much to give you. It's a rich and meaningful exchange that you won't regret. Stay curious as I have so much more for you to discover. Allow Me to use your abilities to study, synthesize, and articulate as a means to reveal the wonders of My creation, the expansive world of one's imagination, and the truths of My love and presence in the world.

Type Six

I invite you to be free from the fear of uncertainty and the false notion that you must be watchful and diligent to assure your protection from harm. You are safe with Me. I am a faithful God who will always be with you. I won't let you down, even in the hardest of times. But you have to rest and trust in My love. Give Me your worries and then let them go. I offer you freedom from the weight of responsibility you carry to do everything right and cover every possible contingency. You won't think of every possible problem and everything will turn out okay in the end. You will feel less stress and anxiety if you accept that things will go wrong. Trust that you will know what to do when it happens. Take courage and be strong.

Appreciate and care for your treasured relationships. Enjoy them, but don't depend on them to make you feel secure or guide your life. Consult Me first. I'm your true guide and strongest foundation. You can count on Me to lead you and support you. No one else knows you or loves you like I do. Keep working hard, serving well, and carrying whatever responsibilities I entrust to you. Allow Me to demonstrate My constancy and faithfulness through you to a world of people who are afraid and uncertain.

Type Seven

I invite you to be free from the fear of being limited and cut off from what you think will give you life to the full. Embrace My love for you and trust that you will not miss out on the abundance I offer. I am with you in all situations. I am the One who redeems all things and turns sorrow into joy. Accept your life as it is now and find wonder in the simple pleasures that surround you. It's really fun to live that way and you will see Me more there than in all the possible experiences you dream of having. Have faith that I will direct your steps and lead you to the places and people I specifically design for you.

Don't run from your hurts, disappointments, and sadness. I will heal and transform these painful emotions if you allow Me into those frightening and uncomfortable places. Your life will be richer and broader if you face the difficult side of life with an open heart to what I will show you there. Reclaim your true self as a reflection of My limitless joy and abundance, and keep being curious. There is no end to what you will discover. Use your hunger for fulfillment and delight to bless others with your zest for life, your love for adventure, and your willingness to embrace the suffering of My world and My people so you can be My instrument of joy and new possibilities.

Type Eight

I invite you to be free from the fear of being unprotected and vulnerable. I will guard you with My love. Let go of the false idea that you must stand your ground and have your way to maintain control over your life. You don't need to display your forcefulness to appear invincible, because you're not. Admit your weaknesses and reveal your struggles. It's the only way you will have access to My true strength and power. Trust Me to protect and defend you, even when you feel vulnerable and powerless. I am your guard. Don't hold back your tender emotions for fear of being hurt. Your true friends will love you more if you let them see the soft and wounded part of you that hides behind your self-protective mask.

Acknowledge that I have gifted you with a passion to fight injustice and release My people from binding oppression and unfairness. My heart of mercy and compassion motivates you to stand in solidarity with those who need a helping hand to rise above the circumstances that hold them back. Keep doing the hard work of speaking up and inspiring others to be channels of change. But don't mix this calling with your own needs to act tough, look strong, and be in charge. Let My strength and power flow through you as a demonstration of My love and care for all people in all situations.

Type Nine

I invite you to be free from the false belief that you don't matter and believe that your place in the world is crucial to the unfolding of My purposes. I see you, and the passions I've given you are worth pursuing. Stop listening to the expectations of others and listen to My love for you. Pay attention to your inner life and develop an ear to heed the small voice within you. Your feelings are important and you'll be a more complete person if you don't dismiss them as irrelevant. They have something to show you. Know deep down that we are in union with one another and I care about every part of you.

Acknowledge that I have gifted you with composure and the ability to go with the flow. It's a refreshing and calming influence in the midst of an uptight world. Please don't use it as a way to hide and ignore what's going on around you. Show up. Access your talent for seeing all sides and help people listen and accept the value of other points of view. I need you to engage in the demanding work of encouraging people to be in harmony with Me, with themselves, and with one another. It's the only way true peace will happen.

Section Four

PRACTICING A PATH TO FREEDOM

10

IT'S TIME TO OWN-UP

"When He [God] talks of their losing their selves, He means only abandoning the clamour of self-will; once they have done that, He really gives them back all their personality, and boasts (I am afraid, sincerely) that when they are wholly His they will be more themselves than ever."
—C. S. Lewis, *The Screwtape Letters*

Having understood our human dilemma, set the biblical foundation for using this tool in our spiritual journey, and explored the Enneagram structure and the nine types, it's time to put it all together and consider how it can be practiced in everyday life.

The process of letting go of our seed coat and allowing space for our true self to grow involves an internal shift that is usually quite subtle, yet powerful. Riding a bike serves as a good example of how a small change can make a big difference. When climbing a hill, even an experienced bike rider wastes a great deal of energy if the gears are too high and he or she must strain to keep going. The rider gets out of breath, wobbles to maintain balance, and gets off to walk the rest of the way if the pain or effort is too much. By adjusting the control lever a slight amount to switch gears, a more comfortable stride can be found to make it up the hill.

In a similar way, when we operate from the Adapted Self, we spend a lot of unnecessary energy and strain. Emotional, mental, and relational difficulties are common. We find ourselves in repeating cycles of the same old habits, as if our wheels are spinning but we aren't going anywhere. As we have seen in the descriptions of the nine types, there are many reactive manifestations of this false-self living: resentment, pride, deception, envy, greed, anxiety, gluttony, shamelessness, and indolence, to name a few. This way of living creates a state of being "out of balance" and "out of breath," like trying to climb a hill in the wrong gear.

The subtle shift of letting go and relaxing into the sacred space of the Authentic Self brings with it a new sense of well-being and more freedom to become the unique image-bearer of the divine nature. We become more receptive to God, others, the world, and our truest self. By releasing the outer seed coat, we allow more room for the Holy Spirit to transform our inner person so it can emerge and blossom. Life is lived with more ease, peace, and fruitfulness, both inwardly and outwardly.

The shift may be subtle, but it's not easy. It requires intentionality, self-awareness, and honest transparency. This shift may occur in a brief moment or during a more extended time of prayer and reflection. In order to describe the movement from a state of reactivity to a state of receptivity, I created a simple acronym that's easy to remember: OWN-UP—Observe, Welcome, Name, Untangle, and Possess. This involves "owning up" to our distorted beliefs and our habitual ways of being that stem from our protective persona as well as "owning up" to the divine gifts of our true self in Christ. It clarifies what we need to "disown" as we seek to follow in the ways of Jesus. This is not a static five-step formula for spiritual success, but rather a way to adjust the internal gears to allow more space for God's transforming work and to experience a smoother ride along life's journey. Once you become familiar with it and practice doing it, it's easy to use in the midst of everyday life.

In the following chapters, I will describe the five elements of OWN-UP and offer some suggestions on how to incorporate this self-awareness process in situations that incite overreactions in you.

I even include some hand motions to depict each step. OWN-UP is most useful if you already know your dominant type. However, it can also assist in determining your type if you aren't sure yet. Here's a quick overview, and then I'll fill in more details:

O is for Observe. This means simply to pause and take note of what you're thinking, feeling, and doing in a given situation and to create curiosity about what these reactions might mean.

W is for Welcome. Like opening your door to friends, this involves welcoming what you've observed as a messenger of something important to know about yourself, even things you may be reluctant to see.

N is for Name. This takes noticing a little deeper what might be underneath your thoughts, feelings, and behaviors. Thoughtful reflection is required to name your inner experience as best you can and peer through the personality microscope to name how your *Eews* and your *Wows* are playing out.

U is for Untangle. This step further identifies what is specifically tangling you up and how to loosen its hold on you. Confession, disowning, and reckoning your old self dead are part of this phase.

P is for Possess. This involves quieting down your inner story and noticing what fills the space opened up by untangling and letting go. By taking claim to your Authentic Self as a unique image-bearer of God and holding to the truth of your life in Him, you can step more fully into the freedom you possess as His beloved one.

To illustrate how this works, I've included a personal journal meditation about a time when I applied OWN-UP in a real-life situation. To assist you in practicing this path to freedom, I've included a simple OWN-UP worksheet on page 189 and a more comprehensive Reflection Journal on my website (www.marilynvancil.com).

Before I unpack OWN-UP more thoroughly, please keep in mind that this is not a step-by-step, linear how-to process. It's more of a dynamic flow that initiates a shift of your internal gears so you can experience more freedom from your false self, more freedom of your true self, more freedom to live fully, and more freedom to love deeply. It's a practical way of responding to the invitation of Jesus to "disown yourself, take up your cross, and follow Me."

11 | O IS FOR OBSERVE

"Your visions will become clear only when you can look into your own heart. Who looks outside, dreams; who looks inside, awakes."

—*Carl Jung*

"There's a lot of fear connected with the inner journey because it penetrates our illusions. Taking the inner journey will lead you into some very shadowy places. You're going to learn things about yourself that you'll wish you didn't know. There are monsters in there—monsters you can't control—but trying to keep them hidden will only give them greater power."

—*Parker Palmer, from "Leader to Leader" Seminar, Fall 2001*

This first phase of the OWN-UP process is to *observe* yourself in action, especially in situations that trigger a noticeable, and often undesirable, reaction. It's like the first step in the scientific method: making a list of observations that evoke questions and curiosity about what they might indicate.

In a similar way, noting your emotions, thoughts, actions, and body sensations provides good data for perceiving a deeper story inside you and perhaps how your Enneagram pattern is influencing your reactions. You step outside of yourself and consciously notice what you are doing, feeling, and thinking. Then you literally or mentally jot down some bullet points describing what you've observed, lingering with them for a moment to become more aware and present to what you're experiencing.

Simple statements like "I feel sad," "I can't stop thinking about this," and "My stomach is in knots," are examples of how observations of your internal world might be expressed. Or "I just yelled at the driver next to me," "I said yes to something I don't want to do," or "I keep checking to make sure the stove is off," are examples of noting external actions. Lastly, habitual patterns could be noted by statements like "I struggle with feeling insecure at church," "I resent people who have it all," or "I'm always angry when my plans have to change." Obviously, there is no end to the possible observations you could make, but the point here is to note the ones that signal an overreaction in a particular situation or repetitive responses that keep surfacing. This stage is not meant to be conclusive. It's the practice of simply noticing and asking "Hmm?"

The ability to watch oneself is called the Inner Observer or Witness by many spiritual teachers. Since we tend to go through life with a limited awareness of our habitual patterns and automatic reactions, this capacity to observe ourselves is often asleep and ineffective. The discipline of regularly pausing and paying attention to ourselves is not something we're very comfortable doing. After all, it might reveal things we don't want to see about ourselves and we might need to change, disrupting our normal mode of doing life. And most of us don't even know how to do it in a way that's life-giving rather than discouraging and condemning. I'm hoping to change that for you. So the first step in the OWN-UP process is to wake up the Inner Observer in order to access its wisdom and assistance on the transformational journey.

Coming out of a deep sleep is not always easy. For me, it usually happens in one of two ways . . . a gradual awakening or an unexpected jolt, like gently stirring in the morning or being jarred out of sleep by an alarm clock or bad dream. Waking up the Inner Observer includes these two primary methods. One is planned and thoughtful, and the other is disruptive and jarring. Both are important.

The first involves paying attention to yourself with intentionality. This could take the form of reflective prayer, journaling, reviewing your day, or pausing occasionally to "check in" with yourself. The point is to nudge the Inner Observer to life and become aware of how you are responding to life. You might notice patterns of thoughts or emotions that keep cropping up, like resignation, envy, or fear. Physical states of your body, like a clenched jaw or restless sleep, become more obvious when you stop long enough to observe them. Reviewing recent behaviors can bring awareness to the ways you try to gain approval, ensure safety, or exert control. This intentional reflection can be about current reactions or personal struggles that have been long-standing.

The second way to wake up the Inner Observer is to consciously take note of what causes an abrupt reaction in a situation. It's like a fire alarm going off, signaling a problem that needs attention. Examples might be an onslaught of fear, a sudden disdain for someone, or abruptly storming out of a meeting. The reaction can be external or internal, like a fit of rage or paralyzing anxiety. The list of ways in which we are affected by an experience, a person, a memory, a future event, or whatever comes along in life is endless. Since we usually operate on autopilot and just react in habitual ways, we often miss the valuable chance to take note of the reactions that create disturbances and jar us awake. We can hit the snooze button and go back to sleep, or we can let the Inner Observer help us stop and notice what we're really feeling and thinking.

Again, the purpose of this first step of OWN-UP is to gather information about your reactivity. After recognizing that something triggered an undesirable response in you, stop and consider the following questions: What emotions am I feeling? What thoughts are running through my head? What are my notable actions? Where am I focusing my attention and energy? How and where am I sensing these reactions in my body? And then linger with these observations for a few moments, inviting curiosity about what these might mean to you.

This is not the time for analyzing what's behind or underneath these observations; just observe and wonder. As stated before, this can take place in a brief moment or over a longer time of reflection.

My husband and I were preparing for the arrival of our family for a week together over the Christmas holidays at a rental property. We had two days to buy food, decorate a bit, and plan for our time together. All in all, there wasn't much to do and we had the chance to enjoy a time of relaxation. Yet I was tense and restless. I kept going over the shopping list. I paced. I was irritable and impatient. I played out possible scenarios in my mind, wondering if everyone would be happy with the accommodations and our plans. My chest was tight, my mind wouldn't stop, and I felt anxious and vulnerable.

All of this was happening without my conscious awareness—I was operating on autopilot—until I took some time to honestly take note of what I was doing and feeling. The situation that caught my attention was snapping at my husband over a simple matter, which caused me to step back and wonder what that was all about. I made a list of my reactions, reflected on them, and by working through the OWN-UP process, eventually gained a more peaceful mind, open heart, and relaxed body. This, of course, impacted my own experience of our family vacation, and I'm sure it created a more enjoyable environment for everyone else.

Here's what I wrote in my journal for the first phase of O for Observe:

> I'm anxious. I keep pacing around the house and can't relax. I yelled at Jeff for no reason. I'm trying to figure every detail out. I'm worried about everybody being happy. My neck hurts and my shoulders are tight. I'm not sleeping very well. I'm full of self-doubt and insecurity. I'm afraid of disapproval. I feel angry, but I don't know why. My heart feels closed and vulnerable. I'm tired. This doesn't feel very good. What's this all about?

Notice that at this stage I merely wrote down some bullet points without coming to any conclusions about what was causing these reactions in me. By doing so, I woke up my Inner Observer. This set the stage for some deeper contemplation about how my Adapted Self patterns were getting in the way and how my Authentic Self might have more space to show up and be expressed during our family vacation. More to come about that as we continue on.

Make two circles with your thumbs and fingers and lift them up over your eyes like binoculars. This first phase of OWN-UP is to use your inner binoculars to look closely and honestly at yourself and describe your emotions, thoughts, actions, and body sensations. Nudge your Inner Observer awake and pay attention to what you see.

Let's try this first part. Take a moment right now and close your eyes. Think of a current situation that caused a troubling response in you. Take a few deep breaths and revisit the scene in your imagination. Notice everything you can about your body, your emotions, your thoughts, your feelings, and your reactions around this situation. Here are some possibilities: confused, critical, tense, fired up, scared, sad, resistant, angry, frustrated, open, closed, nervous, restless, anxious, and on the list could go. Also pay attention to what is happening in you right now as you think back on this situation, perhaps what you want to do about it. Write down whatever comes into your awareness without censoring or trying to explain yourself, blaming anyone else, justifying your responses, or pushing the snooze button and ignoring the whole thing. Now just sit with your list for a few moments and be curious about your inner story and what your Enneagram type might have to do with your reactions. Then let it be for now.

As we go through the rest of OWN-UP, I'll encourage you to come back to this particular situation and finish the whole process of self-observation in a real-life experience for you.

12 | W IS FOR WELCOME

"When all kinds of trials and temptations crowd into your lives my brothers, don't resent them as intruders, but welcome them as friends! Realize that they come to test your faith and to produce in you the quality of endurance. But let the process go on until that endurance is fully developed, and you will find you have become men and women of mature character with the right sort of independence. And if, in the process, any of you does not know how to meet any particular problem he has only to ask God—who gives generously to all without making them feel foolish or guilty—and that person may be quite sure that the necessary wisdom will be given."

—*James 1:2-5 Phillips*

"Our normal response to unpleasant emotions is to do whatever we can to push them out of our awareness. Something quite remarkable happens when, instead of following this well-worn path, we welcome them as a guest in the home of our self."

—*David Benner, Opening to God*

The next movement in OWN-UP is to *welcome* these observations with openness and without judgment. Imagine swinging wide the door of your heart to instructive friends who can show you something about yourself you may have been closed to before. This is not our usual way of responding to negative things about ourselves, is it? Though we may be willing to write down the feelings we observe, or even back up and meditate on those feelings, we may not be ready to embrace them, let alone the learning they may bring.

Read the Scripture above again. It describes the essence of this second step with such hopeful words of wisdom. *Welcome. Quality of endurance. Mature character. Right sort of independence. God gives generously without making you feel foolish or guilty.* These words instruct us to receive what we notice about ourselves without judgment or guilt, but rather with faith that God will lead us into greater maturity and freedom in Him. This doesn't mean we accept or condone inappropriate thoughts, feelings, and actions, or stoically bow down to our difficult circumstances. What it does mean is we allow them into our awareness and then open our hearts to God's transforming love and wisdom.

This welcoming stance is not our automatic response when we recognize things that are unattractive in ourselves. We tend to justify our attitudes and behaviors or just accept them as "the way we are." We might slam the door on these intruders and deny their existence. We may pass the blame onto someone else or claim that we somehow deserve to act or feel a certain way. If we do have the courage to admit our reactive patterns, we often layer on guilt and self-judgment, berating ourselves for such undesirable and sinful behaviors and thoughts. We might grit our teeth and adopt a new self-improvement plan in order to conquer these habits. Or we give them to God and distance ourselves from dealing with them. These tactics rarely work and usually serve to close us down. They also ensure that these "friends" will show up again and again.

There's another option. Visualize moving your "binocular hands" down from your eyes to out in front of you with hands open and palms up. Then add a gesture of invitation, gently moving your open hands toward yourself. Recall some of the observations about yourself and say a simple word of welcome to each one. This posture of receptivity is what the second OWN-UP movement is all about. It represents an open heart and mind and a willingness to change. I have found that this simple step of welcoming settles me and brings a new spaciousness for God's transforming love and presence in my life.

This welcoming phase also involves welcoming God right into the midst of our experience. This is different from giving all our negative feelings over to God and hoping He does something with them. That type of so-called surrender can actually be a way of ignoring and escaping from our unpleasant inner experiences, rather than allowing God to be with us in them. For example, if I'm angry at someone and find myself wanting to hurt them, I can pray, "God, take these feelings away from me." Or I can pray, "God, I'm feeling mad and want revenge. I invite you to be with me in these feelings." It may seem like a subtle difference, but I've found the practice of welcoming God into the truth of my experience has been much more transformational than passing my feelings off to Him.

Back to my journal entry about our family vacation:

Welcome anger. Welcome worry. Welcome insecurity. Welcome defensiveness. Welcome tension. I don't like seeing you very much. I wish I could blame someone else for you. But c'mon in. Show me. I welcome you as messengers and reminders of the ways I want to be in control and stay emotionally safe. I welcome this chance to once again recognize my vaporous false self for what it is and how it could ruin this vacation if I let it run wild. Lord, I invite You into all these feelings and please be with me right in the middle of them. Thank You for opening my awareness and for the gentleness of Your Holy Spirit to invite me to a deeper place with You, a more genuine dependence on You, and a more open heart to myself and others.

Now go back to your list of observations. Pause to quiet your mind, open your heart, and relax your body. Breathe deeply. Hold your hands out with palms up and say "Welcome" without any judgment to each of the feelings you observed around the triggering situation. Receive them as friends to guide you along the path to more freedom. Notice your temptation to resist, run away, and close down. Stay with it and press through to a relaxed place of acceptance and anticipation of what you may learn. Invite God to be with you in the midst of your experience and your feelings. Sit quietly and notice if anything changes for you. Take a few moments to write down what you've experienced in this welcoming posture. Again, we'll come back to this as we continue on to the next OWN-UP movement.

13 | N IS FOR NAME

"The man who can articulate the movements of his inner . . . life need no longer be a victim of himself, but is able slowly and consistently to remove the obstacles that prevent the spirit from entering."

—*Henri Nouwen*

After making initial self-observations and welcoming them with openness and acceptance, along with inviting God to be with you, the next step is to *name* what might be underneath the emotions, thoughts, behaviors, and sensations.

There is a Latin phrase, *Nomen Est Numen,* which means "to name is to know." I first heard this from a Benedictine priest who identifies the flowers and trees he sees on his daily walks. He knows their scientific names, including the species and genera. By doing so, he feels he knows them. He understands their structures, seasonal changes, similarities, and differences. He marvels at the intricacy of each one and experiences a deep connection with creation and an awareness of his own presence in the created order. Perhaps that is why God gave humans the privilege of naming the animals, so they would really know them.

To name ourselves is to know ourselves—to identify our internal landscape and put words to how and why we function as we do. Referring to Henri Nouwen's quote above, the ability to articulate our inner world is crucial for our spiritual growth. We can't disown what we don't own. When we can name with honesty and precision the layers of our Adapted Self and its self-protecting patterns, we own up to the truth of the seed coat that keeps us from the full activity of the Spirit of God in our lives and the experience and expression of our Authentic Self. Although we will never fully understand ourselves, we can identify some of the basic qualities, tendencies, and beliefs that affect how we feel, think, and behave. The N step of OWN-UP is to name our inner experience as best we can and recognize how the observations we have gathered are related to it.

There are two essential pieces to the N step: naming both our *Wows* and *Eews*. Recall that our *Wows* are reflections of our divine gifts, qualities of God imprinted on us to experience and express in a unique way. Our *Eews* are manifestations of our attempts to express these in our own limited and distorted ways. By naming both of these, we can recognize how we try to obtain esteem and affection, safety and security, and power and control by our independent and inadequate efforts.

Knowledge of the Enneagram is invaluable in this process. By considering our thoughts, feelings, and actions in light of the dominant characteristics and patterns of our Enneagram type, we gain some clarity as to what is really going on below the surface in a particular situation. For instance, when I take into account what I know about an Enneagram Nine—my core gift, my basic need, my distorted beliefs, my root sin, my primary fear, my avoidances, and my focus of attention—I can "own-up" with honesty and non-judgment. I'm able to distinguish between what arises from my Adapted Self and what is an expression of my Authentic Self. In this way, the Enneagram serves as a tool for confession, both of my *Eews* and my *Wows*. It's here that holy aha moments frequently come to me and when the reactivity I observed and welcomed starts to make sense. I begin to shift from reactivity to receptivity, from being closed to being open, from being unsettled to being at rest. I'll illustrate this more thoroughly in the continuation of my journal entry below.

The Naming phase of OWN-UP requires more time to listen deeply to your inner movements and allow what might be unpleasant and unsettling to surface. Courage to be brutally open and candid with yourself is required, while keeping in mind that this is the path to transformation and greater freedom.

My journal entry:

Lord, how am I trying to express Your image in me through my own efforts? How am I trying to make my longing for peace happen without You? I'm focused on what each person might want, and I'm so worried this time won't meet their expectations. I fear their disappointment or disapproval with the food, housing, schedule, the whole experience. I want to make sure there are no conflicts with them or between them. I don't want to be disappointed either and I see that I want to control what happens. I feel insecure because I can't possibly meet all their needs. This is why I'm fretful and restless and irritable. I'm mad at Jeff for ignoring my anxiety. I'm not confident and I'm not sure I have much to contribute to this time. I want their approval and I don't want any bad feelings. I see my self-absorption and how I am protecting myself. I am striving to make sure everything goes well for everyone, but I'm not even sure what I really want.

I recognize this struggle comes out of my desire for connection, comfort, and unity. I'm just trying to do it on my own. Deep down, I know I can't but I keep thinking I can if I worry and work hard enough. You've given me the gift of peace and a sense of harmony and flow that will help this time go smoothly. I can bring a sense of calm to a houseful of possible chaos. I know they're all tired so I want them to rest. I love our family and I long for everyone to appreciate each other and have a great time together. I can't make it happen the way I hope it does. Lord, I pray that each person would feel valuable and loved as an important part of the whole family. Thank You that my longings for this time are expressions of Your gift of peace, oneness, and harmony. May I freely bring forth these gifts during this vacation.

As you can see, my meditation focused on two main areas: the admission of characteristics of my Adapted Self and the recognition of the longings and divinely given qualities of my Authentic Self. As I was writing this entry, I thought about my Type Nine tendencies. This guided my meditation and evaluation of what might have fueled my initial reactions. As a result, I was able to name specific demonstrations of my underlying need for comfort, my fear of insignificance, my focus on everyone else's expectations, and my inability to know and value what was important to me beyond making sure there was no conflict. I also remembered these reactions were indicators of how I was trying to meet my needs for control and approval, and the burden I felt to make peace happen. I also acknowledged my divinely created *Wows* and how my thoughts, feelings, and actions—even my negative ones—stemmed from my deep longing to experience and express the gifts of God's peace, unity, and harmony imprinted on me.

Let's return to the situation that created some reactions for you. Take a few deep breaths and settle your body, mind, and heart, preparing for the step of naming your experience more clearly. Again, spend a few moments visualizing what took place, how you felt, and what you did. Invite God to be with you in this time of reflection.

Using the hand motions I've described, start with observing through your hand binoculars, move your hands out in front to express welcome, and now make a rectangular shape with your thumbs touching and your fingers touching, like a label. This represents the purpose of the N part of OWN-UP—naming your inner experience with clarity. Putting this step into practice is pivotal and will prepare you for the final two phases.

Below are some suggestions for moving beyond your initial observations to articulating what's under the surface that may have incited your reactions. As I said, this takes more time and thought. I recommend you write down whatever comes into your awareness as you consider responses to the following questions:

- Read the list of your observations. What stands out and grabs your attention?
- Going a little deeper, describe the underlying motivations that affected your reactions and behaviors. The temptation here is to point to the circumstances or the other people involved to explain your responses, as if you really couldn't help yourself. This is not about explaining or justifying; it's about *naming* your inner experience.
- Review the key elements that describe your dominant Enneagram type—divine gift, distorted belief, core need, focus of attention, root sin, primary fear, and area of avoidance. (Refer to the chart at the end of the chapter on your type for review.)
- In light of what you know about the pattern of your Enneagram type, name how it is operating for you in this particular situation. Where were your attention and energy focused? What were you afraid of? What were you trying to avoid? From what and how were you protecting yourself?
- In what ways were you trying to meet your needs for esteem and affection, safety and security, and power and control by your own efforts?
- Name specific ways your feelings and behaviors were attempts to express the divine gift of your Enneagram type, embracing the truth that God has imprinted His image on you in a unique way.
- Close your time of reflection with gentleness toward yourself and gratitude for God's transforming love and grace for you.

14 | U IS FOR UNTANGLE

"O time, thou must untangle this, not I. It is too
hard a knot for me t'untie."
—William Shakespeare, The Twelfth Night

"People suffer because they are caught in their views.
As soon as we release those views, we are free and we
don't suffer anymore."
—Thich Nhat Hanh

We're complicated. We're a tangled web of hardwiring and history, wounds and praises, thoughts, emotions, gut instincts, perceptions and knowledge, blind spots, and brilliance. Even though we may wish to understand ourselves, it's quite impossible to articulate and explain all that we are and all that we do. So how then can we even begin to disown our Adapted Self and move nearer to the freedom of living as our Authentic Self in Jesus once we've observed, welcomed, and named our inner experience?

Picture this: I recently dumped the contents of my jewelry box all over the floor. The necklace chains of various lengths and styles were already in a bit of a mess, and now they were even more tangled up. Initially, I just grabbed the pile and threw them back into the box; this didn't help. When I tried to sort them out, it took quite awhile. The trick was to locate the one or two chains that were binding the rest and jiggle them loose. Once I did that, the other chains loosened up and I was able to make progress on untangling them.

This provides a good description of the next stage of OWN-UP. *Untangle*. It involves narrowing down the list of what we've observed, welcomed, and named in order to sort out what seems to have a choke hold on us. It's identifying where our attention is focused and our energy is directed. These may be different for every situation. For example, in one incident I may be focused on my anger about being dismissed; in another I may be lost in distractions to avoid doing something hard; and in another I may be stuck because I have no idea what I want. Once we recognize the few binding issues, we can loosen the grip they have on us. And other things might fall away too. This step is about releasing a segment of our dead seed coat so there is more space for the real seed of our true self to emerge and grow.

It may be easy to say, but it's not easy to do. And we need to do it over and over again. Remember the words of Jesus. "Whoever wants to be my disciple must deny themselves and take take up their cross daily and follow me" (Luke 9:23). Let's do a quick review of this three-part invitation from Jesus.

First of all, the word *deny* implies disowning a relationship with someone or saying you don't know them. The "self" we're called to deny is the self God didn't create and doesn't know; it's the persona we've made up to get along in the world. It's what I've called the Adapted Self throughout this book. An expanded version of this verse might be, "Whoever wants to be my follower must say *no* to the pretend self, saying, 'I don't know you. You are not the real me.'"

Second, to "take up your cross" means to declare that this made-up self is dead and has no power. It's also to claim the reality of our true self in union with God through the resurrection of Jesus. It's what I've called the Authentic Self. Two foundational Scriptures tell us this truth: Galatians 2:20 and Romans 6:11. "I have been crucified with Christ. It is no longer I who live, but Christ lives in me. The life I live in the body, I live by faith in the Son of God, who loved me and gave himself for me." "Count yourselves dead to sin but alive to God in Christ Jesus." Remember that "sin" means "missing the true goal and scope of life," not the things we do.

Third, Jesus tells us to "follow Him." He invites us to be with Him and be like Him. We are called to adopt the attitude that characterized His life—the attitude of self-emptying, of not grasping, and of letting go—as we read in Philippians 2. It means relinquishing our self-absorbed way of living, disowning our Adapted Self to make room for our roots in God to go down and our Authentic Self to flourish.

Again, this is impossible to do on our own, but Jesus enables us by His Spirit to fulfill what He invites us to do.

So what does all this mean for the step of *untangling?* Hopefully, my following journal entry will give you a sense of it. Please bear in mind that you're reading this through quickly, but it didn't come about quickly for me. I sat with what I had observed and named for quite some time and prayerfully asked God to reveal the "main chain" that had me wrapped up in knots. I listened deeply to what was stirring in me and I waited in stillness. Knowledge of my Enneagram type gave me some options to ponder but not in a restrictive way. And then, all at once, I knew what it was. A holy aha moment.

> The main thing I'm obsessed about is trying to guess everyone's expectations and trying to meet them all. That's really impossible and ridiculous. I'm worried they'll leave disappointed or frustrated. Somehow I think this reflects on me and whether or not they approve of me. I know it's not true, but right now it feels true. All my fears, my insecurities, my doubts are just rising to the surface in the midst of all this worry about what everyone wants.

Once I recognized and confessed my primary focus of attention and how it was draining my energy and affecting me so negatively, I was happy to disown it, claim it as dead, and let it go. As I did, I felt my insides untangle and loosen up. My heart opened, my body relaxed, and my mind settled. And I was ready and excited for our family vacation! The difficult and patient internal work was in the naming and identifying, but the untangling and letting go was liberating.

Lord, I release this compulsion to guess what everyone expects and orchestrate this vacation so everyone is happy. I recognize this comes out of my longing for approval and need for control and that my false self is trying to make it happen by my own efforts. My false self is dead. I disown all the ways I'm protecting myself and not trusting You. I release my expectations for this vacation. I let go of wanting to defend myself and my choices. I let go of my fear of conflict and disappointment. I release my temptation to be discouraged if conflicts do arise or people are unhappy. I have no control over them and their experience. I give You all of this and I open myself to Your transforming work in me during this vacation. Thank You for my precious family and what's ahead in the next few days together.

After this prayer, I felt free and alive. I really did. I wasn't suffering anymore. I draw your attention back to the quote at the beginning of this chapter. "People suffer because they are caught in their views. As soon as we release those views, we are free and we don't suffer anymore." We might think of "views" as opinions, but it can also be the views we have from the vantage point of our false Adapted Self. And when we hold those too tight, we suffer. When we let them go, we are free.

I invite you to pause and return to your story. Again, take some deep breaths. Center your heart and mind and body with openness to God and yourself. I encourage you sit in stillness for a few moments. Then begin the hand motions I've given you. Start with your binoculars, then open your hands in front of you, then make a name tag, and now release your hands out in a gesture of letting go. Can you sense the flow of movement from reactivity to receptivity to release?

Like me, this step of untangling may take an extended time of prayerful reflection. But I encourage you to try it, just to become familiar with it. And you never know, you may enjoy a holy aha moment right now!

To begin, slowly read through your list of observations and what you named in the last exercise, revisiting the context in which you experienced them. Ask God to reveal the main source of suffering and strain for you. Pause and listen to your inner stirrings. Notice responses in your body. As you read, what makes you feel restricted and tense? What grabs your attention? Does a theme surface? What seems to have a stronger hold on you than the others? These are merely suggested questions to ask yourself as you wait for clarity.

Once you have a sense of the "main chain" around your experience, confess the protective pattern of your Adapted Self. Disown it. Claim it as dead. Follow the example of Jesus and let it go. He came to set you free so you could be free indeed!

15 | P IS FOR POSSESS

"Take possession of the land and settle in it, for I have given you the land to possess."
—*Numbers 33:53*

"You are you. Now isn't that pleasant?"
—*Dr. Seuss*

The above wisdom from Dr. Seuss sums up this final phase of OWN-UP. It's simply and profoundly about *possessing* who you truly are as a treasured child of God, created to experience and express His divine image in a unique way. It's owning up to the remarkable gifts God has imprinted on you. It's claiming God's promises and your union with Him. It's the transformative movement from the tangles of the *false you* to the freedom of the *true you*. Now isn't *that* pleasant!

The story of the travails and travels of the Jewish ancestors give us a poignant metaphor of this movement from bondage to liberation. Beginning with the promise God made to Abram in Genesis 12 to centuries of enslavement in Egypt to deliverance through the Red Sea to forty years of wandering in the wilderness to crossing over the river into Canaan, we are reminded throughout the Scriptures that the ultimate destination of the Israelites was to take possession of the land originally promised to Abram, the father of their faith. "Look around from where you are, to the north and south, to the east and west. All the land that you see I will give to you and your offspring forever. . . . Go, walk through the length and breadth of the land, for I am giving it to you" (Gen. 13:14-17).

I love the part of this narrative when the twelve spies checked out the Promised Land. All but two came back with a scary report, saying the land and the inhabitants would devour them. This set in motion grumbling, fear, and rebellion among the people. But Joshua and Caleb encouraged the Israelites by declaring, "The land we passed through and explored is exceedingly good. If the Lord is pleased with us, he will lead us into that land, a land flowing with milk and honey, and will give it to us. Only do not rebel against the Lord. And do not be afraid of the people of the land, because we will swallow them up. Their protection is gone, but the Lord is with us. Do not be afraid of them" (Num. 14:7-9).

Without discussing the historical and political meaning of these Scriptures, there is much to learn if we look at the Israelites' pilgrimage as a picture of our journey from the restrictive Adapted Self to the freedom of our Authentic Self in union with God. In fact, 1 Corinthians 10:6-11 tells us that these stories were given as examples for us on how to live.

The many details and remarkable connections to spiritual truths in this story (as recorded in the first six books of the Bible) are beyond the scope of this chapter. However, those I find relevant to this concluding step of OWN-UP are summed up in three points: 1) the land was promised and given by God, but it had to be possessed one step at a time; 2) God brought them out of slavery to bring them into a land described as a good and spacious place of rest, flowing with milk and honey, and the most beautiful of all lands; and 3) the land was inhabited by strongholds the Lord would push out of their way as they took possession of it. [20]

Over and over the Israelites were told to *possess* the land promised to them, the land that was already theirs for the taking. In spite of all the fears, rebellions, setbacks, and obstacles, they were encouraged to keep moving, to keep putting one foot in front of the other with faith that God had given it to them.

In the same way, this step of OWN-UP is a reminder to *possess, possess, possess!* Claim ownership of the innumerable promises given to you by a loving and gracious God who desires to be with you and fulfill all your longings. Take hold of the spacious, peaceful, and abundant life that Jesus came to show us and give us. Step out in faith that God will deliver you from all that binds and holds you captive. Possess with confidence the knowledge that the expression of your true and Authentic Self is the imprint of God's image on you.

Why don't we experience this kind of living all the time? Because it's an "already, but not yet" scenario. In Deuteronomy 11:24 God told the Israelites, "Every place where you set your foot will be yours." Yet He also told them in reference to the strongholds in the land, "Little by little I will drive them out before you, until you have increased enough to take possession of the land" (Exod. 23:30). One step at a time. One victory at a time. One segment of our self-created persona dropping away at a time.

Possess. Once we've observed, welcomed, named, and untangled the current situation we find ourselves in, a new spaciousness will replace the restrictive and defensive nature of our reactivity. It almost happens automatically and can't be scripted or predicted. Just as I sensed aliveness and freedom as I released my need to please everyone, more whispers of God's love and presence began to echo in my spirit. As we let go, feelings of peace, clarity, wisdom, joy, faith, hope, love, strength, and wholeness may emerge, to name a few. It's our true and Authentic Self finding expression. This final phase of OWN-UP is to quietly notice what shows up and possess it with gratitude as a gift from God in the present moment. It might be something specific, like an answer to a lingering question, or something more general, like a feeling of settled serenity or assurance.

I offer the final entry of my OWN-UP reflection before our family holiday:

Lord, thank You for Your love and tenderness toward me. Thank You for the peace that is present with me now. I now feel excitement about the days ahead because I can relax and enjoy my family— each one of them. I can freely express the gifts you've given me of calmness and flexibility. May Your love and care flow to them through me. I release all of the details to You. I trust that together You and I will create a rich, meaningful, fun, refreshing, and memorable time. I will carry Your comfort and joy through the coming days. Thank You. Amen.

I invite you once again to return to your own reflection. Sit quietly and review what you've experienced so far, what you've observed, welcomed, named, and untangled. As you take a few deep breaths, bring your hands together in prayer near your heart and listen deeply to what is present for you in this moment. What feelings arise in the space of your open heart and mind? Allow whatever comes to settle in you as a gift from God in this moment. Take possession of your life with Him and the promises of His constant presence. Own-up to the true you—a treasured expression created by God to experience and express His image in a unique and holy way. And give thanks. Amen.

A Summary of the OWN-UP Process

Observe

Briefly describe the triggering situation.
Take note of your actions,
thoughts, emotions, and body sensations.

Welcome

Receive the experience and observations
without judgment, explanation, or justification.
Open yourself to God's presence and love.
Be curious.

Name

Identify the underlying motivations.
Consider the key elements of your Enneagram pattern.
What core needs are you trying to meet in this situation...
esteem, affection, safety, security, power, or control?
Where is your focus of attention directed?
What do you fear?
What are you avoiding?
What is the divine gift of yourEnneagram type?
How are you trying to express it in this situation?

Untangle

What causes the most tension and restriction in you?
Identify what seems to have the strongest hold on you.
Gently loosen and disown what comes into your awareness.
Relax.

Possess

Notice and receive what emerges as you let go.
Identify any new feelings, thoughts, and body sensations.
Affirm your true identity as God's Beloved.
Express gratitude to God.
Rest.

16 | CLOSING REFLECTIONS AND PRAYERS

I began this book by sharing four words that describe how my knowledge of the Enneagram has been a valuable aid in my spiritual life with Jesus: comfort, compassion, confession, and consent. I'm wondering if these same words capture your experience as well.

Are you comforted by a clearer comprehension of why you feel how you feel and do what you do? Is it a relief to know there are other people who view life through a similar lens and wrestle with the same shortcomings and personality quirks? Are you encouraged that your very real and Authentic Self, divinely designed by God, is pushing through the layers of your protective persona and longing for expression?

Have you grown in compassion and gentleness toward yourself as you've discovered the limited ways you strive to earn esteem and affection, ensure your security and safety, and maintain power and control over your life? Are you able to hold your underlying fears, avoidances, and ways of suffering with tenderness and non-judgment?

Has your compassion and care for other people expanded, knowing they suffer and struggle with a deeper inner story beyond what you know on the surface? Do grace, patience, and forgiveness have more room in your spirit because you can appreciate and accept a view of life through the lens of someone else?

What about a need for confession? As the Enneagram microscope revealed both the positive and negative characteristics of your Enneagram type, did you recognize ways you protect yourself and attempt to be your own god? Are you able to more frequently pause and "own-up," knowing that honest and intentional self-awareness is a primary avenue toward experiencing the freedom Jesus promised? Are you able to admit and address specific ways you fall short of God's intended purpose for you?

Lastly, and most importantly, are you more certain than ever that your only hope for change is by consenting to God's transforming work in your life? Only God can set you free from the traps and tangles of your personality. Only God can heal the wounds of loss and misperception. Only by God's Spirit can you fully embrace the invitation of Jesus to disown yourself, take up your cross, and follow Him. As you consent to God and gain courage to release the outer covering of your Adapted Self, your roots will go down deep into the soil of God's love and presence and your Authentic Self will come forth, blossom, and produce a lasting harvest, both in you and for the world.

Comfort, compassion, confession, and consent. As a benediction of sorts, I offer you the following prayers of confession and consent for each Enneagram type. May they serve as a beginning to your Enneagram journey, a reminder along the way, and an encouragement that God is leading you into a good and spacious land of abundance, one step at a time.

Prayers of Confession and Consent

Type One

Lord, I confess I'm attached to my need to be perfect and I believe the lie that my self-created standards earn Your love and acceptance. I confess that I attempt to meet my desire for power and control by over-correcting and judging rather than depending on You. I confess my resentment, disappointment, and condemnation of myself and others when I see imperfections. I disown all the ways my Adapted Self tries to earn my worthiness and protect me from criticism. I claim that my innate desires and abilities to make all things perfect are expressions of Your true rightness and goodness, and I am grateful for the gifts You have bestowed on me. Lord, I surrender to Your transforming love and presence; only You can make me whole and complete.

Type Two

Lord, I confess that I'm attached to my need to be needed and believe the lie that my selfless service is what makes me loveable and valued. I admit that I try to meet my desire for esteem and affection by over-helping rather than depending on You. I confess my pride and the false belief that I must take care of everyone else and not myself. I disown all the ways my Adapted Self tries to earn love and protect myself from the shame of my own neediness. I claim that my abilities to nurture and care for others are expressions of Your true and unconditional love and I am grateful for the natural gifts You have bestowed on me. Lord, I surrender to Your generous and unfailing love; only You can satisfy my longing to be loved for who I am.

Type Three

Lord, I confess that I am attached to my need to be successful and I believe the lie that my value is determined by what I accomplish and how I appear in the eyes of others. I confess that I attempt to meet my need for esteem and affection by over-working to gain respect and accolades rather than believing You love me apart from my performance. I confess I'm deceitful about my shortcomings and limitations and I easily boast about my achievements. I disown all the ways my Adapted Self protects my tender heart by dismissing my feelings and avoiding failure. I claim that my ability to envision brilliance in each person and my gifts of leadership are expressions of Your hope and vision for a bright and better future. I surrender to Your unfailing love and empowerment; only You can fulfill my longings for significance and bring about Your holy purposes for the world.

Type Four

Lord, I confess I am attached to my need to be unique and I believe the lie that I am not enough just as I am. I confess that I attempt to meet my longing to be noticed by striving to stand out and appear exceptional on my own, rather than trusting that I am already special because You created me that way. I confess that I am envious of other people because I think their lives are more satisfying than mine and I want what they have, making me discontent with the ordinariness of my everyday life. I disown all the ways my Adapted Self tries to protect my heart by being overly dramatic or melancholy, creating an intense emotional climate. I claim that my gifts of appreciating the beauty and depth of life are reflections of Your creativity and sacred touch on all You have made for us to enjoy. Lord, I surrender to Your loving and holy presence; only You can satisfy my deepest longings to be special and enough.

Type Five

Lord, I confess I am attached to my need to perceive and know, and I believe the lie that having enough knowledge will fill up my inner emptiness that only You can fill. I confess that I attempt to meet my desire for safety and security by being self-sufficient, detached, and overly prepared. I confess that I fear running out of resources rather than trusting You to supply me with abundance for every need. I disown all the ways my Adapted Self tries to protect my heart by retreating into the private world of my mind and attempting to sort life into categories that I can comprehend. I claim that my gifts of insight and keen understanding are reflections of Your wisdom and light. Lord, I surrender to Your generous love; only You can satisfy my deepest longing to know the truth that will set me free.

Type Six

Lord, I confess I am attached to my need to have certainty and security in my life. I believe the lie that I must do my duty, act responsibly, and obey orders to ensure that I will be safe. I confess that I rely on others to protect me, tell me how to live, and give me assurance that I am okay. I confess that I worry about what might go wrong and spend my energies preparing for the worst that could happen. This keeps me from trusting that You are with me and that You will provide all I need when I need it. I disown all the ways my Adapted Self puts up a guard around my heart and mind so that nothing will harm me. I claim that my gifts of dependability, perseverance, and loyalty are reflections of Your faithfulness and courage. I surrender to Your constant presence; only You are trustworthy and can meet my deepest longings to be safe and certain.

Type Seven

Lord, I confess I am attached to my quest for excitement and adventure in order fill my life with only pleasurable pursuits. I believe the lie that I will be happy if I always have something to anticipate, I'm not limited, and I keep a positive attitude. I confess that I keep my mind busy with plans and dreams so I can keep the harsh realities of life out of my awareness. I don't want to see my dark side or feel painful emotions. I confess I fear being trapped and deprived and resist whatever threatens my happiness. I hold on to my freedom to do whatever I find appealing and stimulating. This keeps me from trusting You as the one who satisfies my deepest longing to experience all that life holds. I claim that my gift of optimism and my abilities to imagine possibilities for a future without suffering are reflections of Your true joy and abundance. I surrender to Your gracious presence in my life; only You can redeem and make me new and fulfilled.

Type Eight

Lord, I confess that I am attached to my drive for power and influence in order to protect myself from being controlled or hurt by others. I believe the lie that I must hide my weaknesses and show my strength to survive in this unjust and merciless world. I confess I fear I might be taken advantage of if I let down my guard or let anyone see my soft side. I hold on to my independence and self-reliance so I don't need to depend on anyone else to defend and care for me. This keeps me from trusting You as my protector and the one who holds my tender heart with compassion and kindness. I claim that my gifts of passion to stand against injustice and my abilities to empower those who are powerless are reflections of Your strength and glory. I surrender to Your gracious and tender love for me; only You can set me free from my own chains of oppression and heal my wounded heart.

Type Nine

Lord, I confess I'm attached to my need for comfort and peace at any price so I dismiss my desires as insignificant and not worth considering. I confess I become lost in the expectations and agendas of others at the expense of listening to You and trusting that You have an important role for me to play in the world. I confess it's easier to be inattentive and indolent than focused and engaged. I admit I inwardly hold on to control of my life and fear I will become invisible if I fully surrender to You. I forget You want me to be the whole and authentic person You designed, which means I matter to You and You see me. I claim that calm and easygoing nature is an expression of Your peace and Your desire for all people to live in union with You and in harmony with one another. I surrender to Your holy purposes and care for me: only You can supply my longings for inner serenity and significant work in the world.

AMEN!

FINAL THOUGHTS FROM THE AUTHOR

Thank you for joining me on this journey. Let's not bring it to an end yet as I would love to hear from you! Here are a few ways we can connect:

Share with me what you've learned and what has impacted you by contacting me through my website at www.marilynvancil.com. Ask me some questions. Let me know if you need help identifying your Enneagram type or want to know about other resources.

Subscribe to my blog and receive details about any upcoming workshops. Also, get the best price on my book by ordering directly from the publisher through my website. Orders of five or more will receive a bulk sliding discount.

Consider meeting with me for spiritual direction or coaching. This can be in-person or via a free Internet service. I offer an initial complimentary session so you can experience what it would be like to work together.

Invite me to facilitate a "Now I Get Me" or "Now I Get You" workshop on the Enneagram with some friends, your work team, at your church, or other settings. This can be introductory or more in-depth, depending on the knowledge level of the group.

Help me organize an "OWN-UP Retreat" in your area to take the material to a deeper level of individual reflection and shared experiences. There is nothing like getting away from a normal routine to listen to God, yourself, and others on a similar path.

Host a book party and mini-workshop to spread the word to your family and friends. If you fill a room with a minimum number of potential enthusiasts, I'll cover my travel costs.

These are just a few possibilities...perhaps you have some ideas too. Again, I'd love to hear from you and learn how I can serve you and others in your life.

Many blessings...Marilyn Vancil

THE ESSENTIAL ENNEAGRAM TEST

This test is intended to be used in conjunction with *The Essential Enneagram* by David Daniels and Virginia Price. Following are nine paragraphs that describe nine different personality types. None of these personality types is better or worse than any other. Each paragraph is meant to be a simple snapshot of one of the nine Enneagram types. No paragraph is intended to be a comprehensive description of an individual's personality.

Read the descriptions and pick the three paragraphs that fit you best. Number these paragraphs from 1 to 3 with 1 being the paragraph that seems most like you, 2 the paragraph next most like you, and 3 the third most like you. Each of the nine paragraphs may describe you to some degree, but choose the three that seem most like you. In making your selections, please consider each paragraph as a whole rather than considering each sentence out of the context of its paragraph. Ask yourself, "Does this paragraph as a whole fit me better than any of the other paragraphs?"

If you find it difficult to choose the three paragraphs most like you, think about which description someone close to you would select to describe you. Because personality patterns often become most prominent in young adult life, you may also ask yourself which one of these patterns would best fit you in your twenties.

After reading the paragraphs and selecting the three most like you, record the three paragraphs you selected and refer to the last page to find the corresponding type. Your dominant type is likely one of these three. For more help determining your type, refer to the type descriptions in this book or in *The Essential Enneagram.*

A. I approach things in an all-or-nothing way, especially issues that matter to me. I place a lot of value on being strong, honest, and dependable. What you see is what you get. I don't trust others until they have proven themselves to be reliable. I like people to be direct with me, and I know when someone is being devious, lying, or trying to manipulate me. I have a hard time tolerating weakness in people, unless I understand the reason for their weakness or I see that they're trying to do something about it. I also have a hard time following orders or direction if I do not respect or agree with the person in authority. I am much better at taking charge myself. I find it difficult not to display my feelings when I am angry. I am always ready to stick up for friends or loved ones, especially if I think they are being treated unjustly. I may not win every battle with others, but they'll know I've been there.

B. I have high internal standards for correctness, and I expect myself to live up to those standards. It's easy for me to see what's wrong with things as they are and see how they could be improved. I may come across to some people as overly critical or demanding perfection, but it's hard for me to ignore or accept things that are not done the right way. I pride myself on the fact that if I'm responsible for doing something, you can be sure I'll do it right. I sometimes have feelings of resentment when people don't try to do things properly or when people act irresponsibly or unfairly, although I usually try not to show it to them openly. For me, it is usually work before pleasure, and I suppress my desires as necessary to get the work done.

C. I seem to be able to see all points of view pretty easily. I may even appear indecisive at times because I can see advantages and disadvantages on all sides. The ability to see all sides makes me good at helping people resolve their differences. This same ability can sometimes lead me to be more aware of other people's positions, agendas, and personal priorities than my own. It is not unusual for me to become distracted and then to get off task from the important things I'm trying to do. When that happens, my attention is often diverted to unimportant trivial tasks. I have a hard time knowing what is really important to me, and I avoid conflict by going along with what others want. People tend to consider me to be easygoing, pleasing, and agreeable. It takes a lot to get me to the point of showing my anger directly at someone. I like life to be comfortable, harmonious, and for others to be accepting of me.

D. I am sensitive to other people's feelings. I can see what they need, even when I don't know them. Sometimes it's frustrating to be so aware of people's needs, especially their pain or unhappiness, because I'm not able to do as much for them as I'd like to. It's easy for me to give of myself. I sometimes wish I were better at saying no because I end up putting more energy into caring for others than into taking care of myself. It hurts my feelings if people think I'm trying to manipulate or control them when all I'm trying to do is understand and help them. I like to be seen as a warmhearted and good person, but when I'm not taken into account or appreciated, I can become very emotional or even demanding. Good relationships mean a great deal to me, and I'm willing to work hard to make them happen.

E. Being the best at what I do is a strong motivator for me, and I have received a lot of recognition over the years for my accomplishments. I get a lot done and am successful in almost everything I take on. I identify strongly with what I do because to a large degree I think your value is based on what you accomplish and the recognition you get for it. I always have more to do than will fit into the time available, so I often set aside feelings and self-reflection in order to get things done. Because there's always something to do, I find it hard to just sit and do nothing. I get impatient with people who don't use my time well. Sometimes I would rather just take over a project someone is completing too slowly. I like to feel and appear "on top" of any situation. While like to compete, I am also a good team player.

F. I would characterize myself as a quiet, analytical person who needs more time alone than most people do. I usually prefer to observe what is going on rather than be involved in the middle of it. I don't like people to place too many demands on me or to expect me to know and report what I am feeling. I'm able to get in touch with my feelings better when alone than with others, and I often enjoy experiences I've had more when reliving them than when actually going through them. I'm almost never bored when alone because I have an active mental life. It is important for me to protect my time and energy and, hence, to live a simple, uncomplicated life and be as self-sufficient as possible.

G. I have a vivid imagination, especially when it comes to what might be threatening to safety and security. I can usually spot what could be dangerous or harmful and may experience as much fear as if it were really happening. I either always avoid danger or always challenge it head on. My imagination also leads to my ingenuity and a good, if somewhat offbeat, sense of humor. I would like for life to be more certain, but in general I seem to doubt the people and things around me. I can usually see the shortcomings in the view someone is putting forward. I suppose that, as a consequence, some people may consider me to be very astute. I tend to be suspicious of authority and am not particularly comfortable being seen as the authority. Because I can see what is wrong with the generally held view of things, I tend to identify with underdog causes. Once I have committed myself to a person or cause, I am very loyal to it.

H. I am an optimistic person who enjoys coming up with new and interesting things to do. I have a very active mind that quickly moves back and forth between different ideas. I like to get a global picture of how all these ideas fit together, and I get excited when I can connect concepts that initially don't appear to be related. I like to work on things that interest me, and I have a lot of energy to devote to them. I have a hard time sticking with unrewarding and repetitive tasks. I like to be in on the beginning of a project during the planning phase, when there may be many interesting options to consider. When I have exhausted my interest in something, it is difficult for me to stay with it, because I want to move on to the next thing that has captured my interest. If something gets me down, I prefer to shift my attention to more pleasant ideas. I believe people are entitled to an enjoyable life.

I. I am a sensitive person with intense feelings. I often feel misunderstood and lonely because I feel different from everyone else. My behavior can appear like drama to others, and I have been criticized for being overly sensitive and over-amplifying my feelings. What is really going on inside is my longing for both emotional connection and a deeply felt experience of relationship. I have difficulty fully appreciating present relationships because of my tendency to want what I can't have and disdain what I do have. The search for emotional connection has been with me all my life, and the absence of emotional connection has led to melancholy and depression. I sometimes wonder why other people seem to have more than I do—better relationships and happier lives. I have a refined sense of aesthetics, and I experience a rich world of emotions and meaning.

Corresponding Types with Test Paragraphs

Paragraph	Enneagram Type
A	Type 8
B	Type 1
C	Type 9
D	Type 2
E	Type 3
F	Type 5
G	Type 6
H	Type 7
I	Type 4

ENDNOTES

1. A more comprehensive explanation of the history of the Enneagram can be found in *The Enneagram, A Christian Perspective* by Richard Rohr and Andreas Ebert (New York: The Crossroad Publishing Company, 2002), 3-21.

2. John Ortberg, *The Me I Want to Be: Becoming God's Best Version of You* (Grand Rapids, Michigan: Zondervan, 2010), 148.

3. M. Robert Mulholland, *The Deeper Journey* (Downers Grove, Illinois: IVP Books, 2006), 23-24.

4. David Benner, *The Gift of Being Yourself* (Downers Grove, Illinois, IVP Books, 2004), 15.

5. Dick Staub, *About You* (San Francisco, California: Jossey-Bass, 2010), 30 and 35.

6. Mulholland, *The Deeper Journey*, 3.

7. Thomas Keating, *The Human Condition: Contemplation and Transformation* (New York: Paulist Press, 1999), 13.

8. Suzanne Zuercher, *Enneagram Spirituality: From Compulsion to Contemplation* (Notre Dame, Indiana: Ave Maria Press, 1992), 22.

9. Karl Barth, Church Dogmatics, Volume IV, The Doctrine of Reconciliation, Part 2 (Peabody, Massachusetts: Hendrickson Publishers, Marketing, LLC, 1958), pg. 538-539.

10. Judith Hougen, *Transformed into Fire: Discovering Your True Identity as God's Beloved* (Grand Rapids, Michigan: Kregel Publications, 2002), 63.

11. Cynthia Beorgault, *"The Wisdom Jesus: Transforming Heart and Mind—a New Perspective on Christ and His Message"* (Boston, Massachusetts: Shambhala Publications, Inc., 2008), 64.

12. Rohr, *The Enneagram: A Christian Perspective*, xxiii.

13. A. W. Momerie, *The Origin of Evil* (public domain).

14. Michael Mangis, *Signature Sins: Taming our Wayward Hearts* (Downers Grove, Illinois: IVP Books, 2008). Mangis uses this phrase "signature sins" throughout his book.

15. Ortberg, *The Me I Want to Be*, 14-15.

16. Richard Rohr, *The Naked Now: Learning to See as the Mystics See* (New York: The Crossroad Publishing Company, 2009), 125.

17. For more information on the Selah contemplative community, refer to the website at www.selahcenter.org.

18. Don Richard Riso and Russ Hudson, *The Wisdom of the Enneagram: The Complete Guide to Psychological and Spiritual Growth for the Nine Personality Types* (New York: Bantam Books, 1999), 13.

19. Rohr, *The Enneagram: A Christian Perspective*. Rohr refers to the redeemed and unredeemed states of the nine types throughout his book.

20. Deuteronomy 1:8, 11:14; Joshua 1:3-5; Exodus 3:8; Ezekiel 20:6; Deuteronomy 6:23 and 12:9-10; Exodus 23:27-30; and Joshua 23:5.

Contact Information

To order additional copies of this book, please visit
www.redemption-press.com.
Also available on Amazon.com and BarnesandNoble.com
or by calling toll-free 1-844-2REDEEM.
Also available through www.marilynvancil.com.

CPSIA information can be obtained
at www.ICGtesting.com
Printed in the USA
LVHW032305310519
619819LV00004B/4/P

9 781683 140382